For Bea

# For Bea

◉

*The Story of the Beagle
Who Changed My Life*

Kristin von Kreisler

JEREMY P. TARCHER/PUTNAM
*a member of Penguin Group (USA) Inc.*
*New York*

While the author has made every effort to provide accurate telephone numbers and Internet addresses at the time of publication, neither the publisher nor the author assumes any responsibility for errors, or for changes that occur after publication.

Most Tarcher/Putnam books are available at special quantity discounts for bulk purchase for sales promotions, premiums, fund-raising, and educational needs. Special books or book excerpts also can be created to fit specific needs. For details, write Putnam Special Markets, 375 Hudson Street, New York, NY 10014.

Jeremy P. Tarcher/Putnam
a member of
Penguin Group (USA) Inc.
375 Hudson Street
New York, NY 10014
www.penguin.com

Library of Congress Cataloging-in-Publication Data

von Kreisler, Kristin.
For Bea : the story of the beagle who changed my life /
Kristin von Kreisler.
p.   cm.
ISBN 1-58542-222-3
1. Beagle (Dog breed)—California—Mill Valley—Anecdotes.
2. Human-animal relationships—California—Mill Valley—Anecdotes.
3. von Kreisler, Kristin.   I. Title.
SF429.B3V66     2003                    2002045181
636.753'7—dc21

Printed in the United States of America
1   3   5   7   9   10   8   6   4   2

This book is printed on acid-free paper. ♾

BOOK DESIGN BY AMANDA DEWEY

This book, of course, is
*for Bea.*

But it's also for another greatly
cherished friend:
*Ray Kilduff.*

WITH LOVE AND THANKS.

Our task must be to free ourselves by widening our circle of compassion to embrace all living creatures and the whole of nature in its beauty.

ALBERT EINSTEIN

Not to hurt our humble brethren is our first duty to them, but to stop there is not enough. We have a higher mission—to be of service to them whenever they require it.

ST. FRANCIS OF ASSISI

# Contents

*Foreword*

Until I read this heartwarming book, I was not confident that a dog who had lived her entire life in a research laboratory could ever reenter the world she was meant to live in — a world of trust, fidelity, and above all, love. But that's just what Kristin von Kreisler's adorable beagle did. Kristin's experiences convinced me that, yet again, in certain areas, dogs and perhaps other animals are our emotional superiors — that is, they feel certain emotions more deeply, more intensely, and more purely than do many of us.

Bea's chronicle was no one-way street where woman rescues dog and dog shows gratitude. Quite the contrary: Bea also rescued Kristin. Through their interaction, both dog and human were able to emerge from their respective shells, proving that love is answered by love. There is no greater power. And when we are willing, as Kristin was, to allow that love to spread beyond our own immediate species, the rewards are extraordinary.

Reading Kristin's account of Bea's life is like listening to a beloved aunt tell you a story you will remember for the rest of your life. If you liked beagles before, you will love them now. I urge you to clear your evening of other plans, sit down, as I did, with this precious book, and stay until you have finished. Be forewarned: Tears and laughter are highly likely!

— Jeffrey Moussaieff Masson
author of *When Elephants Weep*
and *The Nine Emotional Lives of Cats*

# Introduction

You know how some-times your life can seem to turn into a jungle of complex-ities? You worry that just one slight lurch of your wheel of fortune and everything could fall apart? That was how my husband John and I were feeling. After fifteen happy, stable years of marriage, we were living in upheaval. The truth is, we were scared.

I had just quit my tenured college-teaching job to be-come a freelance writer. Though I had published a few magazine articles, I was obsessing over the possibility that I might not sell more. Most days, all day long, anxiety nib-bled tiny pieces from my stomach. Most nights I lay there, blinking in the dark.

For Bea

John wasn't doing very well either. A chemical engineer, he'd just left a secure job in a research lab to join a large Silicon Valley consulting organization, where he had only a few months to prove his worth or he'd be out. He worried constantly about the risk he was taking. While I was blinking in the dark at night, he was tossing in bed and grinding his teeth.

Also, to make it easier for him to commute, we had to move. Just *talking* about moving, without even reaching for the phone to call a realtor, made us feel lonely and up-rooted. For all our married lives, we'd lived in Mill Valley, California, a small town near San Francisco, at the base of a mountain with forests and winding roads and charm. We were about to lose all that, to say nothing of our beloved neighbors, who brought us casseroles when we were sick and who loyally guarded our house when we were on vacation.

Our house was our nest, where we had intended to live forever. Now, because of a vague midlife restlessness, everything was changing. *We* were changing. The question of whether we'd succeed or fail hung in the air above the shark fin of insecurity that circled us and added to our stress.

Of course, our anxieties spread to our animals. At night our German shepherd, Ludwig, barked at branches scraping the rain gutters in the wind or at mice sneaking around in the periwinkle, sounds that in the past he'd have ignored. Tigger, our usually voracious tabby kitty, picked at her food like a fussy restaurant critic and left piles of un-eaten ocean whitefish in her bowl. Whenever John and I sat at the table after dinner and discussed healthcare plans or carpools, Ludwig and Tigger hid in the bedroom to escape the tension, which emanated from us in curly waves. Agitation had become our frequent dinner guest, and the animals knew it.

□

ONE OCTOBER NIGHT, to escape the stress, John and I took Ludwig for a walk. In contrast to our worry, the evening was serene and beautiful. After months of fog curling over the mountain, an Indian summer had turned the air balmy and drawn out the rich scent of bay trees. Crickets chirped, and dogs' barks echoed through the valley as we walked along under a silver moon.

Ludwig, his nostrils flaring with little snorts and puffs, sniffed each message left by other animals along the road. As he bent down to decode a message in a crack in the asphalt, his collar clinked against his leash. Ahead of us, off to the right of the road, a rustling sound came from a clump of brush. It could have been a raccoon, 'possum, porcupine, deer—even a rattlesnake. Whatever it was, Ludwig wanted a bite out of it. He reared up on his hind legs, lunged at it with all his German-shepherd strength— and nearly yanked John facedown on the pavement.

John yanked back. He shouted, "SIT!"

Suddenly a body shot out of the foliage and dashed across the road into more brush. Ears and a tail flew in the air. Paws flew over the pavement.

In the moonlight, if I squinted, I could make out the body of a dog—black and tan and white. Subtract the white and you might have army camouflage. The dog ran out of the brush and zigzagged from one side of the road to the other; she didn't seem to know in what direction to run. But she was desperate to escape us—especially Ludwig, who rattled his leash and whimpered as he tried to control his urge to chase.

The little dog, clearly aware that she was just the length of a leash from battery, tore down the road away from us, ran up a driveway, then raced back down. Obviously confused, she leapt into a patch of nasturtiums, found they were too low to the ground to provide enough cover, and scrambled down into a dark gully.

"That dog is lost," I said.

"I'm sure she's not," John replied. "She's just out enjoying the night the same as we are."

"You're just making excuses because you don't want me to bring her home," I said.

"We don't always have to be the Humane Society."

"We wouldn't *be* the Humane Society. We just have to find out where the dog belongs."

"Let somebody else take care of her. We don't have time." John sounded put-upon and tired.

He could have argued endlessly, of course. But although John surely must have wished at times that I were different, he'd learned to live with my undeniable drawback: I was a pushover, a quivering violet, a sucker for needy animals. I could not bear to see them lost or suffering or scared.

John and Ludwig waited patiently on the side of the road as I climbed down into the gully after the dog. Crunching over redwood fronds, I found her cowering beside a metal culvert. She looked smaller and even more vulnerable than she had on the road. She crouched down, silent, as I approached, and refused to look at me.

Very slowly I bent down toward the dog, so that from her perspective, I would not look like such a giant.

"Don't be afraid." I tried to make my voice a dog biscuit, a pillow by a warm hearth. "I'm not going to hurt you."

The dog, apparently, did not believe me. I patted her head gently, and, in self-defense, she rolled up into a pill-bug ball and tucked her head close to her belly.

Under my hand, I could feel the dog tremble. When I touched her side, a picket fence of ribs told me she was scrawny. No gentle talking on my part could soothe her, and petting made her trembling escalate to vibrating.

Though I was so well-meaning, my hand was obviously her enemy.

I gently scooped up the dog, who weighed about as much as Tigger, and cradled her against my chest, then climbed back to the road. As I moved around bushes and tree trunks, the dog, on her back, flopped her legs out so they bounced up and down, limp, with my footsteps. Without even a flinch of resistance, she accepted being carried; but her heart pounded against mine, and shivers of fear moved, like ripples in water, down her fragile body.

■

AT HOME, I set the dog down on the kitchen floor, and John locked Ludwig in the bedroom. While Ludwig scratched the carpet and sniffed and snorted at the crack under the door, Tigger dashed into the closet to avoid our visitor.

The kitchen light was even less charitable to the little dog than the moonlight had been. She was a beagle, we realized. As she stood averting her eyes and shaking, her personal adjective seemed to be "pitiful"; her personal infinitive, "to huddle." Meanwhile, John was standing at the door with his arms crossed over his chest, a safe ten feet away to keep from getting emotionally involved.

We'd never seen a dog so scared. Or in such bad condition. Her back swayed like a saddle above her squat legs, and her vertebrae jutted out, sharp, beneath her skin.

If a dog could be said to have posture, hers was decidedly poor. Truth be told, she was slouching.

I took her sweet face in my hands and looked into her brown eyes, which were the sad kind that could melt hearts in seconds. She closed her eyes to keep from looking back at me. From their inside corners, streaks of black ran toward her nose, dark paths stained by tears. A wrinkle, which on a person might have formed from constant worry, crossed her forehead.

Perhaps she'd been worrying about her babies, whose existence was obvious from her breasts. They left no doubt that she'd just had pups and was still a nursing mother. Not just the beagle's teats, but also the whole pink flaccid folds of her breasts, hung down, so all the skin and flesh covering her chest swung like a single pendulum. She was surely desperate to find her pups again, but I didn't point this out to John, who was probably worrying that those pups would somehow end up in our house, just as their mother had.

I did point out to him, however, her three redeeming features: Sprinkled on her white-stocking legs were endearing freckles, and at the tip of her tail was a charming whorl of white fur, like an exceptionally unruly cowlick. And her ears . . . well, they were so sensuously velvety that dog lovers might have stood in line to have the chance to pet them. A warm cinnamon brown, they flopped below her chin.

As I turned over one of her ears to rub my thumbs across its exquisite softness, I noticed that it had been shaved inside, and the fur was starting to grow back. In the fuzz I discovered a string of blue, tattooed numbers about half an inch high.

"She's got an ID number!" I shouted, then regretted my exuberance because I'd startled the dog. She trembled even harder.

"Wonderful," John said.

"I can call the SPCA tomorrow. They'll know where she belongs. I can find her home."

Relief replaced some of the distress on John's face.

The tattoo helped us turn a corner from worry to hope, and the tension in our kitchen seemed to dissipate. Possibly sensing a lull in the stress, Ludwig quit pawing behind the bedroom door, lay down, and seemed to accept that we had a temporary houseguest. The quiet made the beagle shake less.

◧

THAT NIGHT, I lay blinking in the dark, as usual. But what I was worrying about now was the beagle. How could I give her back to someone who didn't take good care of her? What was morally right to do with this animal?

I didn't know then that I had years of worry ahead of me — difficult, yet supremely rewarding, happy years. Our houseguest beagle was going to change my life. Ten minutes earlier or later on the road that evening, and I'd have missed her.

But a force far greater than the dog or I was silently at work, a force which has taught me again and again that there's no such thing as an accident, that most things happen for a reason, and that small events can sometimes have huge consequences. Because I met that pitiful little beagle on the road, from that night on, my life would be divided into before and after. And so would hers.

# 1

# My First Mistake

Benjamin Franklin once said that "houseguests are like fish; they start to smell in three days." I have to admit that our houseguest beagle's smell became apparent on our very first morning together. The smell was not literal, of course, though beagles do have a subtle, yet distinctive doggy aroma that I would grow to love. Rather, the "smell" was psychological, an accumulation of little signs that added up to just one thing: Our houseguest dog was riddled with intensely troubling problems.

Honestly, I hardly knew what to do with her. For one thing, she had no inkling of bathroom hygiene. When I came into the kitchen to greet her on her first morning with us, I found her sitting on the bed of towels I'd plumped up into a nest for her. Across the room by the sink lay a puddle vast and deep enough to drown a daddy longlegs. Near the oven was another puddle, smaller, but equally disheartening.

I knew that these were no ordinary accidents because several times during the night I'd gotten out of bed and walked the beagle to a patch of earth near the garage. Instead of taking advantage of the opportunity, she'd stared into the forest with complete incomprehension about the purpose of our trip. No matter my urging, she did nothing. Clearly, no one had ever taught her propriety in toilet habits. Even Ludwig seemed to be repulsed by her lack of refinement.

Another of the beagle's problems was that she would not eat. As I mixed kibble with Ludwig's favorite canned chunky chicken and zapped it in the microwave to produce an irresistible smell, the beagle lay on her towels, with her breasts spread out in front of her like a small rug, and ignored me. I set the bowl of food down in front of her, but she gave it a sideways glance and turned her head to the wall without even a cursory sniff.

She'd eaten nothing since we'd found her; and she continued her fast even when I offered her food in my hands, made ridiculous lip-smacking noises, begged her, talked about the importance of proper nutrition for nursing mothers, and mentioned starving dogs in Ethiopia. She would not drink water either. When I put some beside her, she seemed too upset and suspicious of me to take even a small slurp.

Also, and even more oddly, the beagle wouldn't bark. When a Pacific Gas and Electric Company meter-reader appeared in our yard, Ludwig, who'd been carrying on a feud with this man for years, jumped up and lunged at the window. While the man shot our big shepherd dark looks that threatened Mace, the beagle lay there in eerie silence. And she hardly seemed to notice when a doe came along and nibbled some miner's lettuce outside our fence—while Ludwig went wild on the deck and tried to persuade her to leave.

I could understand the beagle having no urge to protect our house. She surely thought there was no sense getting worked up over the safety of what, to her, was an unfamiliar, temporary shelter. But her not being carried along in the spirit of Ludwig's barking spoke volumes about how withdrawn, and even depressed, she was. She seemed to have no sense of canine packs or the exciting sport of harassing invaders, and an urge so instinctive as barking had been squashed out of her. I hadn't thought it was possible for a dog to be so quiet and detached.

And she wouldn't even consider connecting to me. No matter how hard I tried to befriend her by talking to her and fussing over her, she showed only indifference seasoned with fear. When I went to pet her, she braced herself to receive my touch, then merely endured it.

Otherwise, it was as though I didn't exist. She never so much as stole a glance in my direction.

That, naturally, prevented us from having any kind of decent conversation. Dogs usually "talk" plenty, with yips and whimpers, and convey whole paragraphs of meaning with tail-wags and leaps into the air. But conversation is a two-way street, and our interaction was going in just one direction: me to her. Since she would have nothing to do with me, you could say that, sadly, we were not on speaking terms. With quiet dignity, she stayed to herself in her own private world.

Though I knew I should be above such things, I felt hurt. That didn't stop me from taking her for a walk, however. Then I discovered her biggest problem: Her fear was pathological.

When we set out on the road, she seemed at first to be curious. With her teats scraping the pavement, she tugged me along with the iron will of a stevedore. But once we got to the home of my neighbor Lou, whose dog, Celeste, ran down the driveway yapping squeaky "ruffffs," the beagle's curiosity changed to terror.

Celeste was a pacifist who paraded as a killer, a pygmy mixture of terrier and beagle and perhaps a bit of billy goat. She had a wispy beard. She also had a charming way of standing in a ballerina's pose: feet apart and toes turned out. Even when she tried to act vicious, anyone could see she was a fraud.

For Bea

Though small, Celeste loomed over the beagle. Seeming to recognize that for once she had an edge in size, she stuck her face down in my houseguest dog's and yapped again. Seeming almost to dissolve in fear, the beagle rolled on her back and thrust her legs in the air, as if Celeste were a mighty victor to be placated. The beagle's body language screamed, "I surrender! Forgive me for existing!" If Celeste had been going for an Oscar, she could have set her paw on the beagle's chest and pinned her to the ground.

The beagle's instant submission to such a small impostor of a thug was as awful to see as her fits of trembling. She didn't just shake. She quivered violently like a leaf in a stiff wind. When Celeste's guardian, Lou, came outside to see what all the commotion was about, she took one look at the beagle, narrowed her eyes, and told me that my dog was pathetic—a conclusion I'd obviously reached for myself, but felt was somehow worse to hear from someone else.

When I explained that the beagle was a guest, Lou insisted I should keep her. "Take that dog home and feed her," she said. "You ought to name her Snoopette."

◉

I COULDN'T KEEP SNOOPETTE. I just couldn't. On the other hand, I felt agony at even the possibility of sending her back to an abusive situation. As much as I loved

*14*

John, I was resentful that he, who had rescued so many animals with me before, would never agree to let her stay.

I guess if I were really honest, I would have to admit that I wasn't exactly wild myself about the idea of keeping the dog. But I felt so sorry for her, and I wanted to make sure she had a decent life.

*Bea in the early days*

A wrestling match was going on inside me between my needs and hers. I wasn't capable of deciding the winner.

Finally, I decided to call the SPCA because, no matter what, I needed to know where the beagle belonged. I also decided that I would check out her home before giving her back. Only if the place seemed tolerable would I return her. If not . . . well, I didn't even want to think about it. Not unless I had to. This situation required taking just one apprehensive step at a time.

I left the beagle on her towel-nest in the kitchen, where, I was sad to see, her imagined brush with death in Celeste's driveway had set her back to huddling in her fearful, pill-bug ball. I sat in my white wicker rocking chair, took a deep breath to gather my wits, and dialed the

SPCA. Once connected to the lost-and-found department, I explained that I had found a mother beagle with a tattoo and read the beagle's string of digits from my notepad.

"We don't have any ID number like that registered here." The woman on the phone sounded caring and sincere. "Your dog's number is too long."

"She must belong to someone. What should I do?" I couldn't hide my disappointment.

"You might call the American Kennel Club in New York. They have records for dogs all over the U.S."

On the second ring, a woman at the AKC picked up the phone.

"That's not a regular ID number, lady," she said, her voice like flint. "It's not the kind that dog owners use."

"Then who uses this kind?" I asked.

"Research labs."

My stomach lurched. "You mean this dog is an experimental animal?"

"That's my guess."

My thoughts were racing. This would instantly explain the beagle's heartbreaking condition and put the situation in a whole new league for me. She was no longer just a pathetic, lost dog. After surviving who-knows-what treatment, she'd somehow gotten loose in awful shape in an unfamiliar, terrifying world. More than ever, I had to help her.

"Labs use beagles a lot because they're sweet and friendly," the woman continued. "Beagles are gentle. They don't complain as much as other dogs if awful things are done to them."

I didn't want her to tell me more. I couldn't listen. "Do you have any suggestions about what I should do with this beagle?" I asked.

"You could call around where you live and try to find out what lab she came from. You could give her back."

"I could never give her back."

"Then congratulations, lady. You've got yourself a new dog."

◘

SO, LIKE IT OR NOT, I had a beagle. I kept asking myself, "If not me, who will rescue her?" The answer, consistently, was "nobody." I knew of no one I could ask to take so troubled a dog.

I felt a heavy burden settling onto my shoulders. At first, I resisted it: Why me? Why this dog? Why now? I kept wishing a miracle would come along and take her away, setting me free from moral obligations. I kept wanting to run or to snap my fingers and — poof! — she'd be gone.

But I was stuck. So was John. No matter our reservations, we couldn't turn away from what was being asked of us: a formidable job of giving. The beagle had come into our lives, and we were now responsible for her welfare. We were going to have to do the best we could.

Slowly, though, as with most of life's inevitabilities, I started to accept the beagle, difficult as I was certain she was going to be. I think that somehow, on a deep, fundamental level, I identified with her, as I did with any animal or person who'd had a rocky start in life, as mine had been. It was easy for me to understand how, through no fault of your own, you could be forced to weather a frightening childhood—or puppyhood—and end up shaky. Only luck and love could get you out of it.

The trouble was that I wasn't sure anyone on earth could ever love this beagle out of her bundle of neuroses. She seemed so wounded that she might never come around, learn to trust, and understand that life was good. I could try to coax her back to mental health, but there were no guarantees. And if I failed, then what? I could easily envision years with an animal who would piddle eternally on our carpets and make anorexia her life's mission. As I rocked in my wicker chair and watched her curled up in a dismal heap on the kitchen floor, I saw those years stretch out before me like an empty desert and I had no camel.

In spite of the trials ahead, though, I finally persuaded myself that I could not allow an albatross around my neck to make me stoop. The beagle surely had to have more in her character than fear. Besides her many minuses, she had to have a few plusses somewhere.

The dog closed her eyes and nestled her face against her legs, her rib cage rising and falling with quiet breaths. Now she looked surprisingly peaceful and, though so vulnerable, she also seemed gentle and sweet. I had to admire how she'd gotten through no telling what loneliness and hardship. Any way you looked at her, she was a survivor. Beneath all her anxiety had to lie a bedrock of courage.

As far as I was concerned, this dog had earned the right to be hostile and nasty. Maybe she was justified to snarl at people, howl with malice, or even run in deranged circles. But she did none of these things. On the contrary, she seemed to be a model of acceptance. Calmly breathing in and out like someone meditating, she seemed absorbed in the moment. A Zen monk could have held her up as an example of the practice to live only in the present.

Perhaps John and I had something to learn from her.

◘

I HAD ALWAYS LIVED with animals that were in sterling condition, and I'd come to have no doubt that all animals, if treated well, were good. Oh, I know, there can be mean and surly ones—dogs who nip at the legs of retreating mailmen, for instance, or cats who delight in rolling pencils off desktops. But there can be mean and surly people, too, and, on the whole, I've found that animals tend to be decent. They are usually capable of pure, unabashed devotion that can oil the rustiest of human hearts.

Certainly that had been the case with all of my own animals. Just thinking of how impoverished I would have been without them gave me the shivers. Each animal had contributed to my life in a beautiful way.

As a three-year-old, I would roam around my back-yard in Austin, Texas, with Zipper, our family mutt and my patient companion. He kept me company as I planted corn and watched it grow into stalks that were taller than both of us together. Zipper kept me from learning the meaning of "lonely" until I was older. He was my first real friend.

Fritz, a dachshund who came to my family when I was seven, was my champion and accomplice. He had an amazing ability to defuse family tension. As he trundled around the house on his squat legs or sunned himself in the back window of our salmon-pink, finned Pontiac, he seemed to be on patrol for spats, during which he would rattle his tags to distract the aggressor or just show up and stand beside me, the youngest and smallest in the house.

If I practiced playing our baby grand piano, Fritz's method for deflecting stress was more devious. Whenever I clumped down on a B-natural and a B-flat was required, my mother, a violinist with perfect pitch, would shout from the kitchen, "B-flat! B-flat!" Stung by the harsh tone of her voice, I would silently bite down on the piano's music stand. As an accessory to my crime, Fritz would gnaw on the piano leg so loudly that my mother would run into the living room shouting, "Stop, Fritz! Stop!" Thanks to the distraction he provided, my mother would forget about B-flats for a while, and I could make mistakes in peace.

Sadly, after Fritz became paralyzed in his hindquarters, he was put down. His absence paved the way for a small pride of kitties: Gus, Tommy, and Hattie, who assigned themselves the role of family soothers. As they draped themselves with grace on bookshelves or napped under the skirt of a wing-backed chair, they had a knack for peace and were antidotes to squabbles. They were the calm in my family's storm.

Gus became my personal cat. He would wrap himself around my ankles as I memorized Latin vocabulary words or wrote reports on Texas history. An addict for my lap, he purred like a diesel engine there. At night he slept sprawled over my neck or in my arms with his head on my pillow. By choosing me as his very own, Gus made me feel worthy and important—a very soothing effect, to be sure.

When John and I married, we went to the pound and got Tigger to encourage mice not to use our kitchen as a fast-food restaurant. She was an exemplary employee. A first-class sentinel, she'd sit by the stove in her roosting-chicken position with her legs tucked under her body, daring mice to venture forth. They rarely did.

Tigger also graciously bonded with Woofer, a supremely noble and intelligent German shepherd whom we also adopted. Woofer brought the number in our house to four and made us feel like a real family, not simply a newly married couple with a cat. Most important, for me, was that she became my ardent personal supporter. During my early years as wife and English teacher, she was always there, lifting my spirits with her quiet, loyal presence.

Woofer slept under the table at our first dinner party, and she encouraged me as I graded papers and wrote lectures on F. Scott Fitzgerald. She accompanied me everywhere, like a shadow. Once, when Tigger was lost and I was posting reward signs for her, Woofer waddled along, pregnant, behind me with her tongue hanging from her mouth. Only later, after Tigger was safely home, did I learn that Woofer's pups were dead inside her. Though she must have felt weak and sick, she'd insisted on accompanying me through my anxious search.

*Woofer*

Her dead pups would have become guide dogs: John and I had gotten Woofer from Guide Dogs for the Blind and agreed to bring her back to breed each year, then to turn over her pups.

The last one was Ludwig, who was rejected from service for being high-strung. We adopted him, flaws and all, and he became our proud protector.

Ludwig was a little haughty, I'll admit, and he had his share of quirks, such as a terror of thunder. He could wither us with disdainful looks—especially while walking sideways past his bowl if we'd added too much water to his kibble. But he contributed greatly to our household by seeming to feel personally responsible for keeping misfortune away from us. And when it came to detecting misfortune, his radar was often better than ours.

He despised one of our neighbors. Every time this man jogged by on spindly legs, Ludwig would bark at him as if he were Jeffrey Dahmer. Only later did we learn that the neighbor was a mean, dark-spirited man. But Ludwig had known all along. After that, we learned to trust his judgment.

Now, with a new beagle in the house, Ludwig's tendency to condescend was in full flower. Basically a supercilious human trapped in a stunning German-shepherd suit, he clearly considered this animal to be another stroke of misfortune that he should rout. As he watched the dog trying to make herself invisible on our floor, he made his low opinion of her very clear. His regal bearing, and the scorn bristling like rays from his body, told me that Ludwig felt we had a peasant on our hands, a throwback of a dog, a lowlife with so poor an upbringing that she was the moral equivalent of an ant's toenail. Ludwig was a prince, and the beagle was a guttersnipe, he insisted, and seemed to be waiting for me to request his services as bouncer.

Though I didn't want to disappoint him, he was now going to have to be more like president of the Welcome Wagon. I wouldn't go along with his judgment. On the contrary, I needed him to contribute to family harmony with acceptance of our needy interloper. That was how he could show his decency, if he were willing.

□

BECAUSE OF all my devoted dogs and kitties, I'd come to expect affection to grow naturally between me and nearly any animal I met. All it took was a short chat, I believed, and we would be bonded. Though the beagle was surely the toughest case I'd ever taken on, I expected her to attach herself to me like all the others. Now, after more than twelve hours in our house, she'd had ample time to start to connect. It was time for our relationship to flourish.

I didn't want the closeness just for my own sake; I wanted it for hers, too. I wanted to love her and make up for all she'd been through. I also was eager for her to hurry up and forget her past and understand that she was safe. And I expected to accomplish all this immediately.

Instead of just sitting on the floor with my beagle and waiting patiently for her to get used to me and learn to trust, I got up from my rocking chair and walked across the kitchen to her. My shadow loomed over her like an eagle hovering in the sky above a scared rabbit. She heard my footsteps and sensed that something had blocked the sunshine she was lying in. With a start, she opened her eyes and jumped to her feet.

I stooped down, snatched her up in my arms, and hugged her tightly against my chest. She wriggled and squirmed, then submitted. But hugging her was like hugging a fence post. Even the most callous oaf would have understood that she wished I'd set her down and disappear—forever.

I, on the other hand, was obstinate and determined. I carried the beagle to my chair and tried to hold her on my lap. As long as I wrapped my arms tightly around her, she stayed—how could she have done otherwise?—though her trembling made it abundantly clear that I was frightening her. The instant I loosened my grip, she leapt to the floor and ran back to her sunning spot.

Not realizing that I was being shamefully unfeeling, I told myself that she was simply not getting the point about hugs and cuddles. I was stubborn about wanting to get the joy of closeness through to her immediately, that very day. I patted my knees to call her back to my lap, a demand as preposterous as saying "come" to Tigger. With incomprehension, the beagle blinked at the floor and seemed to shrink even farther into herself.

To say that she was rejecting me was an understatement. Actually, she was avoiding me with every cell in her body. Though she was being polite about it, she obviously wasn't willing to consider even a passing acquaintance, much less a friendship, with me.

That wouldn't do, I thought, and I got up and lumbered back across the kitchen floor to her. With the best but most misguided intentions, I bent down and grabbed her again, carried her back to the chair, sat down, nuzzled my face against the top of her head, and cooed, "Goooooooooood dog."

Terrified, she jumped to the floor and dashed across the kitchen as far away from me as she could get.

With unswerving persistence, I kept trying to hold her in the rocking chair. Again and again she leapt, afraid, off my lap. Each time, she grew more and more mistrustful of me. My efforts to bond were only driving her away.

I gave up. I told myself not to take the dog's rejection personally, though, of course, I'd earned every bit of it. I'd behaved abysmally, I realized, and admitted to myself that her stay with us had been far too short a time to break down her years of hiding, alone, deep inside herself. Our loving bond would have to wait. I didn't know how long.

◘

I WANTED TO GIVE the beagle a name as soon as possible, so she'd have an identity besides the researchers' number tattooed in her ear. A name would make her more a dog in her own right. It might hasten her becoming a being with character and personality and love to give.

As she slept in her patch of sun, I sipped a cup of tea and thought of possibilities. Snoopette was just wrong. Maggie, Lily, Abby, Amy, and Larissa came to mind. None fit. I considered women I admired: Martha Hannon, my mentor, and Mary Prose, my godmother. But Martha and Mary weren't quite right for a beagle either. I tried the names of a few of my favorite women authors—Flannery O'Connor, Emily Brontë, Jane Austen—another dead end. So was "Her," the name of one of Lyndon Johnson's beagles, as were Athena and Dido. This beagle, I felt, needed a modern name.

Discouraged, I gave up for a while. I blew at the steam rising from my teacup and let my mind drift.

Suddenly a thought came to me of a beloved friend, a nun, Sister Beatrice. She'd lived the past five years in a Mexican village, where she'd gone to take hybrid seeds to the *campesinos* and teach them modern farming methods.

Just a week before I'd found the beagle, a friend of Sister Beatrice had called me. "Beatrice was driving up a mountain near her village," her friend said. "I'm sure she was on her side of the road. She was always such a cautious driver."

Her past tense "was" alarmed me. "Did something happen to her?" I asked.

"A truck hit her car," the woman responded. "It crashed down the mountain."

The police had torn the car apart to recover the body. I had been mourning her ever since, one of the finest women I'd ever known, a force for good lost from the earth.

"Beatrice," I said out loud. I knew I'd found the perfect name for my beagle—if only she could outgrow her fear and become as beautiful and loving a soul as Sister Beatrice. To make the name more elegant, I tacked on Louise. That morning my beagle had met Lou, my neighbor—Celeste's guardian. Lou was strong and hardy, qualities I also wanted for my dog.

The beagle raised her head and panted. It was getting warm in the kitchen, and I got up, went over to her, and stroked her head. Naming the dog made her presence in our house seem somehow better, less of an overwhelming imposition.

Beatrice Louise.

I hoped that—with a miracle—she might grow into the name.

2

# The Challenge

I KNEW HER ID NUMBER was too good to be true." John's voice harbored four-penny nails. Just home from work, he looked tired and gray; if his shoulders had been hunched a few more inches, his chin might have rested on his clavicles.

I didn't have to explain that we now had a beagle. He could read it on my face. Though, for the moment at least, I had more or less accepted the dog's presence in my life, what grieved me now was knowing that she—no, let's be honest, *I*—was causing John's distress.

When he approached Beatrice, she cowered; and then as he got closer, just as she'd done with Celeste, she threw herself on her back, raised her legs in the air, and trembled.

But with John, she took her fear another step and urinated, a devastating and unseemly response.

Beatrice was telling us that her greatest terror was
men, perhaps the gender of those who had done research
on her. Maybe I was being dramatic, but as I mopped the
floor with paper towels yet again, I thought of Anderson-
ville, Dachau, the Gulag Archipelago, and the Hanoi
Hilton. Could a dog, like human survivors of those places,
be said to suffer from post-traumatic stress? Was there
any cure for it?

And to see Beatrice so afraid of John, of all men, was
painful. Even as tired as he was that night, he looked dis-
tinguished and handsome. He has fine, patrician features,
like those of a Roman senator on a gold coin. With his
Northern Italian heritage, he also has the genes of those
beautiful, fair-skinned people wearing silks and brocades
in Venetian Renaissance paintings. And John's honesty
and kindness had drawn me to him even more strongly
than his looks. He always keeps people's secrets, sin-
cerely wishes the best for everyone, returns extra change
given by mistake at the grocery store, can be relied on in
emergencies, and is an oak tree of a man. He financially
supported his widowed mother while working his way
through college, and he is a truly gentle person—in other
words, not the type to frighten anyone, and especially not
a beagle, because he loves animals as much as I do.

What might have justifiably disturbed Beatrice were other qualities of John's: He has the practicality of most engineers; he's not going to take on impossible tasks or chase any windmills. He can also dig in his heels and be maddeningly stubborn, and he is responsible to a fault. That makes him worry endlessly about anything important to him, especially the safety and happiness of everyone he loves.

But since we had so many stresses in our lives just then, I didn't think he was about to let himself love or even like a new dog. For now, Ludwig was plenty. I knew John well enough to be certain he felt that way without him uttering a word.

"We have to keep her," I said. "I found out she came from a medical lab."

John blanched and walked out of the kitchen.

I followed him to the bedroom, a better place to argue so as not to frighten Beatrice.

"For all you know, she could have a contagious disease. She could be growing malignant tumors," John insisted. "Have you checked her for catheters? Incisions? Stitches? She could be disabled from experimental surgery."

If he'd said that to make me wince, it worked. So did his pointing out that Beatrice's "barker" might have been surgically removed to keep her quiet in a lab.

"You have to be realistic," John continued. For the

next few minutes, he outlined all the drawbacks of adopting any dog at that time, let alone one like Beatrice. If Lassie had come along right then, John would have sent her on her way. So mentally agile at arguing, he could have been a lawyer. Not me. I just sat there, mute, and searched my brain for verbal ammunition, but my arsenal was empty.

A few years later, I considered writing an article on the importance of animal companionship, and I came across numerous studies about all the good that Beatrice— or any animal—could have done John, especially at such a critical time for him. I could have razed him to the ground with research which proved not only that he should have kept Beatrice, but that he should have felt grateful to her for her potential to help him sail through his job change. The facts and figures about the benefits of being with animals would have appealed to his scientific mind.

Rather than being a source of stress, Beatrice could have calmed John down. I discovered that just watching *fish* has been shown to lower blood pressure. I'd bet that watching a warm-blooded beagle could help even more. In a Brooklyn College study, people were asked to read out loud with or without a friendly animal in the room. With an animal present, their heart rates were lower, another indication of serenity. Researchers at the State University of

New York at Buffalo asked women to count backward by thirteens and seventeens from a four-digit number, a nerve-racking task. Those with their dogs beside them had both lower blood pressure and slower heart rates.

I found numerous studies proving that being with a dog or other animal can make people less prone to the hypertension, infections, and heart disease that stress can bring. An Australian study of 8,000 people showed that the company of animals can even lower cholesterol! If the strain from John's new job ever got bad enough to cause a heart attack, God forbid, he would be more likely to recover because of Beatrice, as I learned from research by professors at Brooklyn College and the University of Pennsylvania. Out of ninety-two people hospitalized with heart disease, only 6 percent of those who had a dog or cat at home died within a year. When you consider that 28 percent of those without an animal died that first year, you can see how beneficial Beatrice could have been to John.

She might even have kept him from needing to go to the doctor for the minor illnesses that occasionally cropped up for him—headaches from commuting, for instance, or lower-back pain from sitting for long hours at his desk. A researcher I discovered at UCLA surveyed 938 Medicare patients; those *without* companion animals visited a doctor 13 percent more often than those with an animal. Fewer hours spent with doctors would mean more time for John to read the *New York Times* and listen to public radio while winding down after work.

As if improving John's physical health were not enough, Beatrice's presence in his life could have improved his mental health, too, just when he badly needed an emotional boost. In a variety of studies I came across, people who shared their lives with an animal were shown to have a better self-image, seeing themselves as self-sufficient, confident, and optimistic. Michael McCulloch, an Oregon psychiatrist I read about, surveyed thirty-one patients, each of whom was contending with a medical illness, but also had a companion animal at home. All of these patients believed that their animals distracted them from worry, made them feel secure, and helped them cope with feelings of loneliness and isolation.

Perhaps all of these psychological plusses add up because of animals' ability to show empathy and unconditional caring. From a United States Army Veterinary Corps national survey of 896 military families with animal companions, I learned that 77 percent of the respondents felt that their dog or cat understood when they poured out their troubles, and 73 percent said they believed their animal communicated back to them. So I could have told John that Beatrice might almost be a therapist, ready to build his confidence or coax him back to equilibrium if he came home feeling out of sorts.

If he took her to work, the benefits of adopting her would mushroom. Specifically, she could improve his image among colleagues and clients. According to a University of Pennsylvania study I found, people appeared less intimidating to others while interacting with their dog or cat, and the tension lines disappeared from their faces. Research by Randall Lockwood at the Humane Society of the United States has determined that someone walking or playing with an animal is perceived as being happier, more approachable, and even more intelligent. As a consultant, what more could John ask for? When Lockwood showed subjects pictures of people in similar scenes with and without an animal in them, those people with an animal, as you might guess, were believed to be more friendly and attractive. With Beatrice sleeping on the floor of John's office, there's no telling how much more smoothly his meetings with clients might go.

In the end, though, I couldn't really blame John for being upset about Beatrice because I still wasn't exactly at peace with her myself. I wanted everything to be better, quickly—without any major confrontation—but all I could think to say that night was the obvious: "We have to keep her. We don't have a choice."

With great reluctance, John gave in. He had one condition, though: Beatrice could stay if Andrew Kallet, our veterinarian, assured us she was in no pain and was healthy enough to have around our other animals. John and I didn't shake hands on this, but we had an agreement.

◘

ANDREW HAD BEEN our dear friend for three years. We'd met him when he was a resident at the University of California at Davis vet school, where we'd taken Woofer, who had systemic lupus, an autoimmune disease. She'd gotten so ill that she couldn't walk, but Andrew managed to get her moving again, and she lived for a year. I would always love him for that gift of time.

After house-sitting for us once, Andrew decided to move to our area. He joined a clinic near Mill Valley, where he soon became widely recognized as smart and competent. Many people had since come to rely on his good judgment. If he'd been a doctor for humans, I'd have entrusted him with my life without a moment's doubt.

But Beatrice didn't trust anything about his clinic. As soon as we arrived, its smells of disinfectants, medicines, and illness triggered another fear attack. Surely she thought that I, with the moral turpitude of Benedict Arnold, had double-crossed her and brought her back to a lab. In the exam room, I kept telling her that I had not, but she clearly did not listen. With her tail plastered between her legs, she checked the smells of the cabinets, tile floor, baseboards, garbage-can pedal, and doorstop. Her sniffing seemed frantic and defensive rather than curious, as if she were looking for what might harm her so she could steel herself for the pain.

When Andrew opened the exam-room door, his white lab coat must have dredged up associations that made her disintegrate in fear. He hadn't taken a step inside before shivers seemed to radiate clear from her bones out through her muscles, skin, and fur. The shivering became so violent that her fur shook in a blur, the way blades in an electric fan rotate so quickly that they look like fuzz. Every inch of Bea's body seemed to be in motion. Of course, she rolled on her back and urinated.

Andrew was very good about it and assured me that dogs were often scared of vets. I could tell from his frown, however, that he'd sized up Beatrice immediately and wasn't exactly pleased by what he saw. He didn't seem surprised when I explained her origins, or by her reticence when he held out his hand for her to sniff. Andrew didn't press the friendship but gently picked her up and put her on his exam table, where her nervous panting was *agitato* and her drool made polka dots on the steel surface.

Slim and athletic, Andrew looked as if he should be out bicycling or kayaking or jogging down the road with Lila, his black Lab. Though he cared about animals, he was sensible about them, like John, and didn't get squishy with sympathy toward them, as I did. He efficiently set about examining Beatrice—taking her temperature, listening to her heart, and examining her ears.

From her scruffy fur and paltry weight, twelve pounds, he determined that the beagle was severely malnourished. Her teeth told him that too, and they told him her approximate age, which, he guessed, was about five years. From a superficial check, he couldn't figure out what she might have been used for in the lab. Whatever it was, he believed that she was now in such bad shape that she might never come around and live a normal life. "This dog could end up being more trouble than she's worth," he concluded.

Andrew wasn't being mean. He spoke in the matter-of-fact tone of a dispassionate observer who was trying to help. "Sometimes lab animals never make good pets," he added. "They can be erratic. They can think everybody's trying to hurt them. Or they won't come out from under the bed, and they'll snap at you if you try to engage them."

If you asked me, Beatrice didn't look like she had a snap in her. But, then, how could I tell? "But she doesn't have anything *really* wrong with her this very minute, though, right?" I prodded.

"No major illness, if that's what you mean."

We discussed, as John had requested, whether Beatrice was suffering or could introduce a medical threat into our house, like some kind of small biological-warfare delivery system. Andrew agreed that on those counts she was fine.

Though he gave a few more warnings, nothing he said

flashed red enough to change my desire to keep the dog. Andrew seemed to accept that Beatrice's somewhat murky bill of health made me even more determined to give her a chance. Though he wasn't exactly supportive, he didn't press his views and was respectful of my decision. I had the feeling that if problems arose with Beatrice down the road, I could call him and not get an I-told-you-so.

Andrew prescribed vitamins and a special, highly nutritious food, a dog's version of Ensure that we hoped would double her weight. Then he picked Beatrice up from the table and set her on the floor. He shook his head sadly and said not once, but three times, like a mantra:

"Used and abused.

Used and abused.

Used and abused."

For months that phrase would echo in my mind.

□

ANDREW HAD BEEN considerate enough not to speculate in detail about the kind of treatment Beatrice might have received in the lab. That would, fortunately, remain vague for me. But it didn't take much for my imagination to paint a bleak and unsettling picture, which, emotionally speaking, was like a blend of Francisco Goya's *Saturn Devouring One of His Children* and Edvard Munch's *The Scream*.

In my mind I could see Beatrice living day after day for years, confined to a tiny cage. She would never have

For Bea

known what might be done to her, never had any way to
resist it when it happened. She would have lain there endlessly with her eyes closed, with nothing to do but hide inside herself and wait for adversity to approach her in a lab
coat. Or she'd have sat with her paws in front of her to
steady herself, staring out at the laboratory through bars.
If her cage had been near the floor, janitors might have
come along at night and accidentally clanged on the bars
with terrifying mops and brooms.

Beatrice might have had just enough space to shift
her weight, lie down, sit up, stand up, readjust her position again and again to fight an overwhelming sense of
being trapped. Probably rarely able to leave her cage, she
must have pawed the floor, shredded her papers (if there
were any) to keep from lying in her urine and feces, and
slept as much as possible to fight the endless hours of bore-
dom. Frustration and depression would have sunk their
claws into her and pierced her spirit. As her mind dulled
from lack of stimulation, food might have become her only
solace.

Perhaps even worse, if she'd been separated from
other dogs for years, she'd probably have grown desolate.
She might have had hazy memories of a mother and sib-
lings; those memories surely would have made her isolation harder. Like a prisoner who'd never committed a
crime, she'd most likely given up, her brain slowly shutting
down in defense against her loneliness. Though she could

not have known that she was missing space, freedom, and a human family who would love her, she must have known that life was tough. She must have felt misery.

When I imagined these things, nothing could have made me turn my back on this dog. The harshness of her life nagged at me; and if I had anything to say about it, the harshness had to be made up for. No matter what anyone said — and in those early days there was a whole parade of friends who told me I was crazy — I could not let this beagle down.

Looking back, my determination may, strangely, have had something to do with an exhibit of my fiber art, "Waste Not, Want Not," which had just opened a few weeks before Beatrice appeared on the road. From friends who were cleaning out drawers, and from thrift shops that were getting rid of inventory, I'd collected cast-off items that nobody wanted and that would otherwise have gone straight to the dump. My neighbor Rorie left a grocery bag of motley pantyhose on the hood of my car. Andrew Kallet donated several past-their-prime T-shirts. My handyman, George, showed up with a box of threadbare bath towels. I dyed many of these nasties, then wove, sewed, or crocheted everything into useful and sometimes even surprisingly beautiful objects. From faded blue jeans and men's out-of-fashion ties, I made quilts; from frayed sheets, rag rugs; from sagging curtains, placemats. Everyone's dregs got a new life.

In an apologia that went with the show, I explained that, as well as simply appreciating the aesthetic challenge of this work, I did it because I liked reviving the pioneer-woman virtues of economy and thrift, and rescuing the downtrodden and pathetic. Most important, I got great pleasure from the wonder of transformation—the alchemy of turning chaff into gold. Each object I made, I felt, meant a "victory for the underdog."

That's what came to me when I decided that, no matter what, Beatrice and I were joined for life: for richer or poorer, in sickness and in health, through puddles and impropriety. I didn't see myself as Beatrice's savior, but more as her Statue of Liberty, ready to encourage her as her ship came in to the hope and safety of Ellis Island. Turning her life around would be another—and literal—victory for the underdog.

I knew that somewhere in Beatrice, no matter how deeply buried, there was treasure. Even if she'd been used and abused, I would not let that hamper her potential. I dug in my heels with new resolve to make her right.

◘

MY IMAGININGS about Beatrice's past were not all depressing pictures of her life in the lab. Often, in her early days with John and me, I wondered about the various ways she might have escaped, and those thoughts were decidedly uplifting.

Sometimes in exuberant, fanciful moments, I pictured her changed into Mighty Dog, crashing through her cage door and charging out of the lab to freedom. Or I saw her, like Peter Sellers in *The Pink Panther*, turning stealth into an art form. She would silently nose open her cage's latch, sneak down the hall to an elevator, and slip in among the grove of passengers' legs for the ride to the lobby, where she would hide behind a wastebasket until she saw the chance to make a break for it.

A beagle on the lam, especially one so emotionally beaten down as Beatrice, though, was not a very likely scenario. The Mighty Dog image didn't exactly jibe with Beatrice's tendency to huddle. The truth was that someone must have helped her escape; and though I would never meet that person, I invented a detailed story of her efforts and played it again and again in my mind. I named Bea's imaginary rescuer Alice and made her twenty-three years old, a university student who works in a San Francisco lab at night to pay her tuition. I envisioned Alice as having frizzy, ash-blond hair and a tender heart that sometimes gets her into trouble. Rarely out of her uniform (Reeboks and jeans), she carries her noodle soup for lunch in a striped, wide-mouthed thermos, and dog biscuits in a paper sack for the beagles whose cages she cleans.

I imagined a scenario in which Alice one day unlatches Beatrice's cage door and reaches inside, breaking the un-written rule that says lab employees must be indifferent.

She has seen Beatrice's gentleness, and her sympathies have gotten the best of her—especially after she's read a lab report and discovered that Beatrice has served her purpose and is about to be put down.

Alice can't steal Beatrice and bring her home to her apartment because of a no-pets clause in her rental agreement. So, she resolves to do what she feels is the next best thing: Late at night, she hides Beatrice under her sweatshirt and dashes to the lab's emergency exit. A feeble light bulb glows at each stair landing, six floors to the ground.

Her heart fluttering, Alice hurries to her green 1978 Volkswagen and sets Beatrice on the passenger seat, where the dog roots around to look for her pups, then presses against the door as if it were her cage's wall. She hardly knows what to do with so much space. Alice starts the car and drives out of the parking lot, and Beatrice calms down but still shivers occasionally while peering out the window.

The orange streetlights are so bright they make Beatrice squint. The sound of passing cars confuses her. When Alice turns corners, the motion makes Beatrice dizzy, then queasy. She trembles at all the strange sensations and smears the window with her nose. Then Alice speeds onto the Golden Gate Bridge, and the car's tires hit the road's seams. The "thuh-thump, thuh-thump" startles Beatrice. She stirs and tries to find a more secure spot to rest her paws on the leather seat.

Alice takes the Mill Valley exit and drives into a canyon of towering redwoods. She slowly steers around a switchback, and the trees grow thicker and block the moonlight. There are no streetlamps.

Away from houses, Alice stops at another turn in the road and walks around to open the passenger door. Beatrice tries to watch her through the windshield. But the shadows swallow Alice's shape, and Beatrice grows more disoriented and frightened.

"Out," Alice whispers, opening the door. "You're free. You're on your own." She sets Beatrice on the road.

Possibly for the first time ever, Beatrice's paws touch something besides a steel table, a cage, or a concrete floor. She takes cautious steps on unfamiliar asphalt and sniffs the mountain air. Unsure of what to do, she circles Alice — Beatrice's only tie to what she knows — and peers around her Reeboks.

"Go on!" Alice shoos the dog away. "I've saved your life. Go find a home!"

Beatrice watches, confused, as Alice climbs back into her car and drives away, leaving a trail of exhaust fumes. Alone in the darkness, the beagle gets a whiff of squirrels, deer, raccoons, cats, and other dogs. Instincts deep inside her come to life for the first time. She presses her nose to the ground and inhales more deeply.

Ahead in the distance John, Ludwig, and I are out for

our walk. At first Beatrice doesn't see or hear us because smells and urges have overtaken her. Aware for the first time in her life of her ability to run free outdoors, she dashes off in search of anything familiar.

And then we see her.

# 3

# Beagle-Civilizing

JOHN WAS NOT HAPPY that we now had a beagle, but to his credit, he was honorable about living up to our agreement. Though Beatrice had barely passed the health test, she was now a member of our family. She was one of us — one of *his*.

In the next few months, her fear of John dictated a respectful distance between them. Nevertheless, his feelings seemed to soften. When he looked at her, his expression became less dour. Though he had first referred to her as "the dog," in a few weeks, that changed to "the poor beast." Then one day he called her Beatrice. And finally one evening, in a triumph of her success at winning hearts, he asked, "Have you fed Bea?"

One morning, I had been feeling discouraged about her puddle problem, and I halfheartedly suggested that we buy stock in companies that made paper towels. John reached across the table and squeezed my hand.

"Bea will get better. Don't worry," he reassured me. "Remember, we're in this together."

I'd longed to hear him say that. To my needy ears, his quiet comment was a Beethoven crescendo with cymbal clangs and trumpet blasts. From then on, John and I spent many evenings over dinner discussing how, together, we could best help Bea, who became something like a 4-H project, a distraction from our other worries. She bound us closer together and got us working as a team.

We formalized our commitment to her by registering her with the county, so she was licensed and proper in the eyes of the law. Then we attended to the various items we felt she needed. We bought her a food dish, a black leather collar and leash, and a brush with fine, curved wire bristles.

Since, by then, the fur in her ear had overgrown her tattoo, we ordered her an identification tag: a metal disk with "Beatrice" engraved on one side, and our phone number on the other. When the tag arrived in the mail, I worked it onto a loop on Bea's collar. Now if she ever got lost, I told her, the tag would turn her into a boomerang: She would always come back to us.

We also bought toys—tennis balls, a squeaky carrot,

a string knot for tugging, and a small, bouncy rubber pyramid called a Kong. No matter how I approached her with these toys, however, Bea either did not comprehend their purpose or was afraid of them. She couldn't grasp the meaning of play. Rolling a tennis ball toward her or holding the knot in front of her mouth made no sense, and she ignored them. When I squeaked the carrot in front of her face, she jumped back; after that, the carrot stayed silent. The Kong lay idle on the kitchen floor.

Bea reacted more positively to a charming wicker dog bed handed down from Moosey, a neighborhood mutt. At first Bea didn't want to step into the bed; but I picked her up and held her on its foam rubber mattress until she understood the pleasure of softness. Then she would regularly lounge around in the bed with what looked like pride of ownership. We often caught her in a proprietary sprawl.

Once Bea had her essential belongings, John and I turned to the next crucial issue: how to get her to be a normal dog. I had never really liked the word "normal" because it seemed elitist, a standard that measured with a single sweep, including some in a cozy circle and pushing others beyond the circumference. Nevertheless, we wanted Bea to be as much like other dogs as possible. We wanted her to be ordinary, average, like the unremarkable but always satisfying flavor of vanilla.

Though John and I never actually sat down and devised a strategy to accomplish this, by trial and error we worked out a beagle-civilizing program. It was three-pronged:

The first prong was getting Bea settled in a strict routine because regularity, we hoped, might help her feel as if life were predictable rather than frightening. We started with her meals: Every morning and evening at exactly seven o'clock, she was given chicken bits with Andrew's special food, and at noon for lunch, three small dog biscuits. In the beginning, food seemed to be almost an affront to her, but gradually she became accustomed to the schedule and the menu. Though she was never ravenous, each day she left less food uneaten, and slowly she gained weight.

At ten and two each day, I took Bea out to the patio to sun herself on the warm red bricks for half an hour. Instead of just lying there, she gradually began to look around and explore. As she grew accustomed to life outside a cage, she made discoveries about the natural world and observed the towhees, finches, and blue jays who frequented our bird feeder. While Tigger lay in wait under a sword fern and nursed delusions of grandeur about her jay-hunting prowess, Bea hung back, her head cocked in curiosity. If the birds flew from the feeder to the roof, she turned her whole body around to keep her eyes on them. She studied butterflies swooping down onto the agapanthus, and hummingbirds dipping their beaks into our feeder's red sugar-water.

Mostly Bea learned about nature on the patio by sniffing. She pushed her nose down into piles of leaves, dirt, redwood fronds, and acorns, and then seemed to inhale not just with her nose, but with her whole body. Drawing smells deep inside herself, she raised her shoulders, pulled in her stomach, and puffed out

*Bea exploring*

her chest. When satisfied, she would move on to another subject with her nose skimming the bricks.

Promptly at 10:30 and 2:30, after these airings on the patio, I brought Bea back inside and set her on a blue denim pillow in my study. I wrote articles and query letters while she napped and often dreamed, seeming to be processing her life experiences: After a few minutes of snoring the "uuuuhhhxxx" of gargled pebbles, Bea would pump her legs as if she were running, or make muffled wheezes. Perhaps in those dreams she chased men in white coats around labs and evened some scores.

Bea's routine seemed to help her become secure enough to start to bond with me—and with John, too, though she was more reserved around him. She acknowledged our presence by glancing at us when we walked into the kitchen. Sometimes she got to her feet, a vague gesture of welcome. She also began to make a few per-functory comments — no lengthy conversations, mind you, but simple, terse statements. She sighed to say that her bed was comfortable, looked up at me to ask for a dog bis-cuit, or nosed her bowl across the kitchen floor to point out that she enjoyed her food. At last we were almost connecting.

The connection, John and I hoped, would be en-hanced by the second prong of our beagle-civilizing pro-gram: taking Bea out into the world and socializing her. This part, supposedly, would familiarize her with real life, help her see that we would keep her safe, and allow us to spend quality time together. And that might ultimately be an antidote to her fears.

I took Bea on rides in the car, and we took walks through the neighborhood and in downtown Mill Valley, where I encouraged her to step on sidewalks, gravel paths, and playground sand. Though she was always hesitant at first, touching such novelties with her paws gradually be-came less threatening. New noises, though, were a differ-ent matter. Bea worried greatly about engine roars, horn honks, and the shuffle of pedestrians' feet, and she never really became comfortable in traffic or crowds.

The hardest but most important part of her socialization was introducing her to people. I started with our neighbors and graduated to gentle-looking women strangers, up to whom I dragged Bea, then explained that I was trying to help her become less afraid of people. "Would you pet her for a minute?" I'd ask. The women would comply, but they often held out their hands with reluctance. Bea was clean and brushed, and even a little pleasingly plump around her middle, but her vibrating was a turnoff.

The beagle-civilizing program's third prong, house-training, was the biggest challenge. Never in all my years had I wrestled with such a problem. John had taken to calling Bea "Old Faithful" because a geyser was guaranteed every hour on the hour. He joked that our kitchen should have a concrete floor with a drain in the middle for easy hosing-down.

I couldn't be so lighthearted. Though I didn't mean to brood over this indelicate subject, I couldn't help myself, because Bea's problem was constant and chronic. There was no escaping it.

The serious training began with Andrew's suggestion that we march Bea outside at least a dozen times each day until she understood what we wanted. Even the marching part was not easy. At the front door, Bea would roll on her back with her legs in the air, a position of passive resistance, which we began to call her Gandhi act. Only after

I pushed her halfway over the threshold would she give in, turn over, and walk the rest of the way. Then I'd take her to her designated bathroom spot by the garage and stand with her—in rain, fog, drizzle, wind, or moonlight. "You can do it!" I'd encourage.

When, by miracle or chance, she did what was asked, I rewarded her with a piece of hotdog, the food that most excited her. "Gooooood Bea!" I'd say, patting her head. But the quid pro quo of the outdoor puddle for the hotdog never seemed to dawn on her. She thought that just walking to the bathroom spot meant snacks. If I brought her back into the house without a hotdog morsel, she looked disappointed, even huffy. I'm sure she believed that I was cruel and erratic, and that she couldn't count on me for anything.

John suggested that I take Bea out with Ludwig, so he could model the desired behavior. Ludwig would sniff the grass beside the road, seemingly indifferent at first, then growing serious. He'd paw the ground and then, with dignity and majesty, raise his leg.

Bea never grasped the lesson. She didn't even pause to think about what Ludwig was doing. When we returned home, she'd look up at me with expectant eyes and remind me that it was hotdog time. "No bathroom, no hotdog," I'd say firmly and, ten minutes later, find a puddle in the kitchen.

Four packages of hotdogs later, Bea still didn't understand. "Maybe her elevator only goes halfway up," my friend Marilyn commented.

The dog-training books I checked out of the library seemed to jeer at my failure. In *The Beagle*, Thelma Gray claimed that when it came to housetraining, beagles were "exceptionally easy to teach to be clean, for all but a minority are naturally fastidious." As if that weren't enough of a slap, Gray added that she constantly met people who told her that beagles were "reliable in an astonishingly short space of time." Well, I wanted to tell Ms. Gray, I was now coexisting with the queen of obstinacy in the bathroom department. Months had passed, and Bea was not reliable at all.

In *Beagles*, Lucia Vriends-Parent made me feel even worse by suggesting that perhaps I had not been alert enough to the signals that Bea might have been sending. Apparently, I should have been watching for times when Bea looked uneasy, sniffed, and walked in circles as if searching for something—and then I should have snatched her up and taken her outside. The book also suggested that perhaps I'd been lax about correcting her whenever she'd had an accident. I was to lead her up to it, point at it, and scold her "in a low, growling tone"—like a wolf, I supposed.

I watched and waited for signs, snatched Bea up, escorted her outside. I growled at her lapses. Alas, there was no progress. The helpful hints did nothing to solve the problem. John and I were just going to have to live with it while we waited for Bea's enlightenment.

◘

WHEN BEA SNIFFED AROUND and explored during her daily outdoor time at ten and two, the neighborhood dogs would arrive, one by one, to inspect her. With grave concentration, they would peer down from the street and watch her on the patio.

First came a husky, Otis. Other dogs had beaten him up occasionally, so his life-is-tough experience had taught him to be cautious. He'd sniff the air and pace back and forth behind our English laurel bushes to get a better look at Bea. Then he'd scratch the earth next to the road with his hind paws and disappear.

Next came Charlie, a mutt whose bloodlines were impossible to discern. Spotted black and white, he'd saunter over from his home across the road and station himself in the flower bed near our mailbox, where each spring he took pleasure in digging up my marigolds. Charlie would watch Bea with the cool, steady stare of a sentry in a castle turret. He was so quiet and unobtrusive that she didn't seem to notice him.

Nor did she notice Snowball, a Samoyed, who arrived

from down the road a few days later. In a blizzard, all anyone would have seen of this dog were his shiny black eyes and nose. The rest of him was dazzling white, fluffy, and graceful. When he trudged along the road, his delicate feet made him seem to prance.

Snowy would stick his black nose into the bushes and shove his head forward to get a closer look at Bea, but he wasn't big or strong enough to push his way through the hedge. He'd move to the water faucet near the garage and sit on top of our coiled hose. Then he stared and stared at Bea as if he were calling her up to the road to play with him. Ignoring him, she'd settle on the bricks to sun herself.

Olaf, a great Dane and lummox, stopped by, as did Sam, a galumphing black Labrador retriever. So did Bear, a Rhodesian ridgeback. And Monte, a local mop-like mutt.

All these dogs were gentlemen callers, and they seemed to be checking Bea out for possible trysts. Rather than bringing billets-doux or bouquets of roses to win her over, however, most of them lifted their legs and marked our gate, an affront that made Ludwig furious.

John and I discussed the possibility of one of these swains getting into the yard and forcing himself on Bea. We agreed that there were already enough beagle pups on the earth, and that she was in no condition for another pregnancy. So I was the designated Judas who got to take Bea to Andrew to be spayed. One morning, before she'd had food or water, I scooped her up, drove her to the clinic, and with great trepidation handed her over to a friendly vet technician, who didn't seem to judge me harshly when I made her promise for the fourth time to take good care of my dog.

As I turned around and left Bea, I felt my heart squeeze. All day, I could not work. I pictured my beagle conked out on an operating table with an anesthesia mask over her sweet face and worried that Andrew might sneeze with the scalpel in his hand.

Sitting poised over the telephone, I waited for Andrew to call with news about how Bea was doing. Finally, late that afternoon, he let me know that he'd not only spayed her, but also done a tummy tuck to keep her breasts from sagging to the floor. The operation had been a success, and it also revealed a clue about her past: Andrew told me that he'd never seen such huge arteries as those going to Bea's uterus. He guessed that she'd been used as a puppy mill, though he had no idea of the number of her babies.

Perhaps researchers had kept her constantly pregnant; or once the experiments on her were done, they'd given her to a breeder, who had used her as a puppy machine. Her past, though, was not nearly so important to me as my present eagerness to get her home; and the next morning I got to the clinic before it opened, and I waited to pick up Bea. At home, I gently set her in her bed. All day long I offered her extra dog biscuits and handled her as if she were Baccarat crystal.

By the time the fur had grown back on Bea's shaved chest, she was shapely and sleek, like other dogs—another small step toward normalcy. As John and I often pointed out to each other, she was progressing little by little.

◘

MONTHS AFTER BEA was spayed, she would still roll on her back and urinate if a man came close to her. John was good about not pushing a relationship, because he wanted her to get over her fear in her own way and in her own time. But when our gentle friend Joe Backus arrived for a visit, he was less patient. He was determined to change Bea's attitude.

Joe, an English professor at the University of Hawaii, was sprightly, slight, and agile from practicing yoga. Deep in his soul there was an elf whom he suppressed during the academic year but set free during time off in the summer. Joe meditated on crystals, communed with spirits, and looked for messages in clouds. Just before he arrived at our house, he'd attended a dowsers' convention in Los Angeles and a shaman conference at the Peace Pipe Lodge in Montana.

When Joe met Bea, the first thing he did was give her a Native American name: Little Dog. Then he made her a God's eye (a shaman's tool) by weaving yarn the colors of her fur over and under two crossed sticks, like filling in a wheel's spokes. He hung the God's eye on Bea's wicker bed to protect her from evil spirits while she slept. Then he set about persuading her that he was worthy of her trust.

Many times each day, he'd squat down beside her in the posture of an Apache by his campfire and whisper, "You're the best, Little Dog." He stroked her ears, head, and shoulders, and patted her stomach. "I only have your good at heart. I just want to be your friend," he softly reassured her.

Bea, of course, could not help herself. Predictably, she'd tremble and go into her submission mode. I'd grabbed so many paper towels by then that I could have cleaned up her puddles blindfolded with my hands tied behind my back. This went on for the whole week Joe spent with us.

Joe refused to view Bea's puddles as negative. He told her they were in harmony with the universe. He insisted they did not express fear, but, rather, ecstasy. And you know what? Bea almost seemed to believe him. Though she still assumed her submissive, wet pose in his presence, she also seemed to stop shaking so dramatically. And when Joe patted her belly, she didn't cringe and withdraw inside herself as usual. Bea actually looked Joe right in the eye, as if she were curious about him. Soon she would some-

times let John pet her without vibrating, too. Though subtle, this step in her development was huge.

She took another big step on the afternoon before Joe
left. We were sitting on the deck in the companionable silence of close friends, drinking a cup of tea, and watching
the redwood trees grow in the backyard. I was glum because we'd just returned from a dismal, fruitless house
hunt near where John worked. While I indulged my discouragement, Tigger dozed in a deck chair beside us and
let out sighs that sounded like air escaping from a bicycle
tire. Bea and Ludwig were on the patio in front of the
house.

Suddenly Ludwig interrupted the quiet with a thun-
derous bark.

"Olaf must be tormenting him at the gate again," I
told Joe. We listened to make sure that Ludwig hadn't
cornered the Pacific Gas and Electric man on the stairs
down to the meter. But Ludwig's barking came from another spot on the patio, so I knew he was just swaggering
around and being macho—perhaps showing off for his
other archfoe, the mean-spirited next-door neighbor. I expected Ludwig to launch into another round of deep-
chested barks, but, instead, I heard a second dog's
high-pitched, delicate yips. They were coming from the
patio too.

Joe and I rushed to the kitchen window and saw Bea

*Joe and Ludwig*

chasing Ludwig. They were playing! As she ran across the bricks after him, she turned her head toward the sky and howled "Arrroooooo!" She yipped staccato phrases that didn't seem to be directed at anything, but at everything in general. They accompanied her dancing. She leapt up and put her paws on Ludwig's shoulder. And then she barked. An honest-to-goodness, undeniable bark. The most beautiful bark in the world. It was light and tentative, but there was no mistaking that Bea was letting the world know she was glad to be alive. She was rejoicing.

That night at supper, Joe and I described Bea's barks to John. They'd seemed almost to physically brush my face in the same way that Helen Keller said she could feel the vibrations of music literally touch her skin at symphonies. Bea's barks seemed somehow more than sound. They felt tangible, as if I could hold them in my hand. They had the hopefulness of stardust. I now knew she would be all right.

"Do you see how Bea meets life with a good bark?

That's what we all should do," Joe said. In other words, I should "bark" at my discouragement about the house hunt, and John should "bark" at his fears of failing at the new job. By barking, Bea showed us resilience, spunk, and bravery at being uprooted. When the students are ready, I learned that day, the teacher will come.

# 4

# Conversations
# with Bea

AFTER JOE BACKUS'S
visit, Bea continued to grow less frightened of men. We
noticed as the days went by that when John approached
her, she would roll only onto her side instead of all the
way onto her back. Her quivering became less frequent;
her submissive puddles, less predictable.

Gradually, Bea seemed almost to forget to be afraid.
John could make tea or prune laurel bushes a few feet
away from her, and Bea would continue to eat, play 'possum, or sniff the patio as if she hardly noticed him. Finally, one afternoon he walked right up to her and patted
her. She didn't beam at him; but she didn't shrink back.

We were so thrilled that we broke all rules and gave her a hotdog without her required outdoor puddle.

That day marked a turning point in our relationship with Bea, and the barrier between us and her seemed to come down as unexpectedly and quickly as the Berlin Wall. Bea lost her reserve, opened up, and began to talk with us. We quickly discovered that she was a skilled communicator—not so much with the precision of Demosthenes as with the homey conviction of Ronald Reagan: She had a knack for getting right to the point of any subject and dousing it with feeling.

With her pleading eyes and insistent yips, Bea could have persuaded Santa Claus to deliver presents in July. We, too, were putty in Bea's paws. Her excited leaps into the air made it impossible not to believe that taking her for a walk right that very minute wasn't just urgent, but obligatory. If she regressed occasionally to the despair of her early days with us, she told us all about it with a droop that seemed to overtake her body, and the feeling was contagious; until she returned to her cheerful self, our whole house would sink into gloom.

To convey quick, uncomplicated thoughts, Bea developed a repertoire of tail wags. The Metronome was her happiest; with her tail straight up, she wagged it rhythmically from side to side. If all the back-and-forth movements of her tail were seen as a continuum, they would form the semicircle that a wiper makes on a car's windshield. Bea used this wag to say "Good morning," or to announce how pleased she was about her forthcoming supper. Sometimes she got so carried away with joy at the sight of her kibble that The Metronome might have been counting sixteenth notes for *Flight of the Bumblebee.*

Less exuberant was The Swish, when Bea wagged her tail in a horizontal line straight out from her spine. She reserved this wag for speaking almost absently or sometimes to no one in particular, like J. Alfred Prufrock wondering if he dared eat a peach, or a vaguely attentive Chekhov character musing on life in the country. We might find Bea lost in thought on the deck, staring into space, and swishing about the coolness of the fog. Or as we made our lunch, she might swish, preoccupied, about her intention to curl up in her basket soon and take a nap.

She executed The Bongo in a sitting position with her front legs propping her up so that her body made a small tripod. Then, with the force of Desi Arnaz belting out calypso, she would thump her tail on the floor or against a wall or kitchen cabinet. She was especially likely to thump when I was preparing a meal or a snack for her. She told me in no uncertain terms to hurry up because she couldn't wait much longer. Patience, she thumped, was too much to ask of a dog.

Because of The Bongo, we began to call Bea our Bongo Beagle, and soon our names of affection for her outnumbered her tail wags. Besides Beeper, Beeps, and Beagle, as we'd been calling her for months, John, a strong and masculine man, took to cooing, "Our Little Beagle Weagle," "My Bongo-Bongo," "My Wee Bee," and "Come here, Little Weeee." I was considerably more restrained. I called her Beepsie, Boogle, Beapy Boo, and Woogle. (When we were addressing Bea in this manner, Ludwig, of course, would walk into the room and assume his Czar Nicholas stance, which seemed to suggest that perhaps the hour had come for Thorazine.)

Bea loved the names and would tell us so as clear as day by perking up at the sound of them, especially at mealtime. No matter which name we bandied about, she seemed to know that it applied to her. When I would call "Beapy Boo," she would raise her head from her basket pillow. "Boogle-Woogle" might bring her to her feet and sometimes get her to walk across the kitchen toward me.

Along with her names, Bea learned other words. As her vocabulary grew, so did her ability to speak with us about other matters. Even whispered, the words "ice cream," for example, would send Bea bounding to me with any number of verbal rejoinders, which all basically boiled down to "yippeeee!" So would "Want to go for a ride?" and "walk." "Walk" didn't have to be part of a coherent sentence to send her into ecstasy. John and I even had to spell out "w-a-l-k" when we discussed taking one. Otherwise, Bea would dash to the front door, where she would emphatically point out her joyful hopes; and we would feel like unbridled cads if we decided not to go outdoors with her.

The other word that really got Bea discussing her dreams and aspirations was "biscuit." We gave her a b-i-s-c-u-i-t whenever we went to bed at night or had to leave her home alone. She could speak for hours about the virtues of Milk-Bones, which, as she explained to me, were her raison d'être. In a daily oratorio, she would count the ways she loved them: for their crunch and flavor and dumbbell shape, and the way they crumbled into tiny bits with just one snap of the teeth. All we had to do was say "biscuit," and she insisted in the strongest possible language that we give one to her immediately.

All these responses from Bea were overt, exuberant public expressions of feeling that she could have been shouting to any number of people. In sharp contrast, Bea also began to have lengthy, private discussions with John and me. They were deeper and more complicated tête-à-têtes of a personal nature, like conversations whispered over a back fence on a summer evening. At these times, Bea would reveal her innermost thoughts to us, and she allowed us really to get to know her.

One of these heart-to-hearts took place when I was soaping up Bea in the bathtub. She had just returned from The Country Inn, where our friend Natalie Apple had kept her for a week while I accompanied John on a business trip to Japan. Of course, we had agonized over whether Bea was confident enough by then to be separated from us. I had spent hours weighing the plusses and minuses of leaving her in a kennel like Natalie's.

The plusses were that Natalie always arranged for her canine guests to receive freshly sautéed chicken at each meal and to be walked out to her meadow twice a day to visit sheep. Also, Bea would have a huge run all to herself right next to Ludwig's, and they would be regularly allowed to play together. In addition, Ludwig adored Natalie and always trotted amiably to her door—and there was no reason to believe that Bea wouldn't develop the same affection. But there were two large minuses: The kennel might remind Bea of a lab and dredge up sorry memories. And the real clincher: We felt strongly that Bea needed us in order to feel safe and secure.

I drove John nearly crazy by obsessing over the decision, but with our departure date looming, I had to make up my mind. John and Natalie kept repeating their primary argument in favor of my taking the trip: Bea might become more self-assured than ever once she knew that she could get along on her own without us. Finally, I agreed. I took Bea to the kennel and, with great sadness, left her.

You can imagine how much I enjoyed Japan. As I meditated on four piles of sand in Kyoto and fed crackers to deer in Nara, I was constantly thinking of my beagle.

Her face, with its neediest, most eyebrow-rumpled expression, haunted me. I felt the way you do when you have a tooth pulled and your tongue keeps going back incessantly to the gap. Sometimes I'd send mental cups of hemlock to John for having persuaded me to accompany him in the first place.

When we returned, Bea greeted me ecstatically—and confidently, just as John and Natalie had predicted. Ahead of Ludwig, she charged into Natalie's office, where I was waiting, threw herself at me, and asserted with vehemence that I take her home immediately. On the ride, though, she grew distant. As Ludwig panted with pleasure at passing cars, Bea sat in the front passenger seat with her eyes fixed on the glove compartment and refused to look at me.

In this way, she quietly announced that while her stay at the kennel hadn't been torture, summer camp it was not. I'd stretched the truth when I'd described it to her as such.

I told her I was sorry. I'd meant well. But she indicated that it would take her a while to decide if she could trust me again. As you might guess, Guilt climbed into the car, sat on my lap, and pinned me to the upholstery.

It didn't help matters that when Ludwig, Bea, Guilt, and I got home, I had to point out to Bea that her odor was unsavory and I was going to have to plunk her in the bathtub. As I lathered her up, I tried to cheer her by talking with her in the friendly way of a hairstylist gossiping with a client over a shampoo. But Bea didn't seem in a gossiping mood, and I quickly saw that I had badly overstepped the bounds of the shaky trust that had so slowly developed between us. Refusing to respond to me, Bea mentioned her hurt feelings. And then, as they say, when it rains, it pours—and Guilt refused to share his umbrella.

Bea's tail said it all. For months, she'd been holding it in exactly the way a beagle is supposed to: curved up cheerfully into a smile rotated a quarter-turn to the side. But now Bea's tail didn't curve at all. She held it straight out horizontally from her body, like "The Swish," except that, halfway along the vertebrae, she bent her tail down into the water almost at a right angle, like the handle of an antique water pump. At first I thought maybe she'd hurt herself somehow at the kennel, but she seemed not to be in any pain. Then I realized the significance: Bea was saying, "No smile on its side for you."

A frank and honest dog, she could not pretend that all was well between us when it was not. I had been extremely unkind, she pointed out. I had lured her to the car for a ride, and then I'd taken her to a barely tolerable place. Though she'd seen worse, "kennel," nevertheless, was a euphemism for "jail." And I had dumped her.

"Oh, please don't say 'dumped,'" I exhorted. "I just dropped you off."

Dumped, Bea insisted. I had abandoned her. She wasn't going to give me an inch of slack in this discussion. She was adamant.

"I didn't mean any harm," I pleaded. Chastened to the core, I hugged her, lather and all, and tried to reassure her that I was deeply sorry. I dared not mention the b-i-s-c-u-i-t that I was about to give her as a peace offering, because I didn't want to have to chase a sodden, slippery beagle from the tub to the Milk-Bone box. I did promise Bea, though, that she would only have to stay with Natalie occasionally, perhaps once or twice a year at most and never for longer than a week. "If we leave, it will always be temporary," I vowed. "We'll come for you the minute we get back."

We'll see, she said as distinctly as any dog ever said anything. She was still holding back her forgiveness. As she gazed at the soap dish and attended to her bruised feelings, I felt stuck between the Scylla and Charybdis of her needs and John's; and I couldn't promise that hers would always win out over his. That would be a lie, and I now knew that Bea was very touchy even about a slight exaggeration, such as my having told her that the kennel would be like a dog vacation.

I kept petting her and lifting her tail to get her to hold it up again—an indirect way of begging "Please, please, won't you forgive me for being so insensitive?" But each time I raised her tail, she let it fall back, emphatically down and out, to the water-pump handle. I dried her off and hung a towel over her back, so she looked like a miniature jousting pony. She then added an extra turn to the end of her tail, so it stuck out from the towel like a Model-T crank.

After her bath, I took Bea to the kitchen and gave her three biscuits to bridge the chasm between us. After that, I'm relieved to say, she lifted her tail back to the sideways smile. I now understood that a beagle, though stubborn, couldn't stay hurt for long. I surely didn't want to test Bea on this observation very often, though, and I was glad that we'd had our talk and cleared the air.

◉

SOMETIMES IN JOHN and my discussions with Bea, we'd all start off in a perfectly calm and rational manner, and then the talk would get ratcheted up to a fiery debate. I may as well rattle the skeletons in our closet and confess to you that we were not always a model family. Occasionally, Bea and John and I got into spats.

The most memorable one was between Bea and John, though it was all my fault, I suppose, because I tend to be overprotective of anyone I love. I had gone out one afternoon to bring Bea in from her scheduled two o'clock sunbath on the patio—and she'd disappeared! When I called her and she didn't come to me, I became frantic.

I searched the bushes around the house and tried to

parry my imagination, but it overpowered me. In my mind, I saw Bea hunted down by a dogcatcher and hauled to the pound in a cage on the back of a truck. The staff would see her metal identification disk and be about to contact me — but then someone would discover Bea's tattoo. Instead of calling me to come and get her, they would turn her back, like a runaway slave, to the laboratory.

My stomach tightened into tiny braids of apprehension. I checked the gate and found it securely closed; then, afraid that Bea might have dug her way out under the fence, I examined it along the house but found no holes. I ran down to the forest behind our house, where Bea had never dared to go, and I shouted "Bea!" until my vocal cords felt like they might fray.

Then I heard something stir in the periwinkle next to the fence. Only the top of Bea's head showed among the leaves and purple flowers. Apparently, she had wandered down to the bottom of the yard and gotten lost. Having lived in a cage for so many years, she had no sense of direction, and she couldn't figure out how to get back to the house. So she had hidden to protect herself, a commendably sensible solution, I thought. What distressed me was that she hadn't come when she'd heard me shout her name, though she must have known I was desperate to find her. And then she didn't even apologize for causing so much trouble. She just wagged The Metronome and said she was glad I'd come for her.

I had the right to be upset, I believed. Though I understood her side of this impasse between us, I felt that my opinion counted as well. And my opinion was that I never wanted to go through a scare like that again. For Bea's own safety as well as my peace of mind, she had to learn to come when called.

But despite my entreaties, John was hesitant to teach her to respond to her name because of his memories of training Ludwig. Sometimes I thought that Ludwig's first obedience class was becoming almost a repressed memory for John. He never seemed to want to talk about it. It had been so hard. We had dragged Ludwig—then six months old—up the sidewalk to our neighborhood recreation center. A chunky Rottweiler of a man had met us at the front door. "What's this big boy's name?" he asked.

"Ludwig," John answered.

"Good boy, Sandbag." The man gave Ludwig's massive haunch a playful whack.

He was the instructor of the class we had enrolled Ludwig in, and he insisted that we buy, right there on the spot, a choke chain for our dog. Ludwig cowered. Somewhere in his universal unconscious must have been memories of choke chains. We cowered, too, because we were reluctant to take such a harsh measure against our vulnerable, sensitive puppy. But the instructor insisted, and we caved. Once outfitted, Ludwig bucked and leapt and went nearly wild when the chain's metal links scraped to-

*An adolescent Ludwig*

gether. John wrangled him to the ground. "Attaway, Sandbag," the instructor said, and then he told us to go inside.

Ludwig may have looked huge and fierce, and his adolescent German-shepherd teeth could appear quite menacing. But in those days he was shy; and when he met all the other dogs and people that crowded into the hall, he hid behind John's knees. "I guess he has to grow up sometime," John said with resignation. In an uproar of howls and yaps, anxiety spread from other dogs to Ludwig, then up the leash to John. Around his eyes, I noticed tiny lines, like craze in china, that I had never seen before.

The instructor climbed onto a wooden platform and shoved his windbreaker's sleeves above his elbows as if he were about to do something unpleasant with his hands. He clapped them together, an absurd attention-getter if you consider the din of barking and wrestling in that room. He told us all to line up our dogs along the mat that circled the hall. Ridges, like tire treads, were embedded in the mat's black rubber. So were toenail marks, the autographs of earlier agitated students.

The teacher smiled with the confidence of a lion-tamer. "When I say 'Go,' tell your dogs 'Heel!' and start walking around the room."

At "Go," the room broke into pandemonium. People said "Heel," shouted "Heel," screeched "Heel." A few precocious dogs followed their guardians like gentle lambs. But not the rest. Some yowled at everyone around them. Choke chains scraped to near-hysteria. Ludwig reared on his hind legs like a stallion gone mad and lunged at the teenage girl in front of him. In terror, she pulled her toy poodle off the mat.

"Down, Ludwig!" John's voice thundered across the hall and seemed almost to rattle the windows. He glared, his face like stone. Whimpering, Ludwig started dragging John toward the hall's exit. On his way, Ludwig snapped at a cocker spaniel standing innocently beside the Birkenstocks of his frail, gray-haired mistress.

"All right, we can't get discouraged!" the teacher shouted, his determination untarnished. John went back to the mat with Ludwig, who, after his shameful assault on the girl and the spaniel, now had more room around him in the ring than any other dog.

For the next half hour, the teacher asked for more "heels" and got more bedlam. More lines appeared in

John's tense and ashen face. Ludwig's own face seemed quickly to lose its puppy innocence. John, his formerly beloved companion, had become his opponent, to be fought every chance he got.

Thankfully, after a couple of weeks, it was finally conveyed to Ludwig that John was the alpha male of their pack. By the end of three semesters of classes, they had worked out a fairly solid truce. Ludwig generally did what John asked, more or less, though considerable browbeating, cajoling, and scrapping still continued between them on occasion.

To persuade John to take on Bea, I emphasized his great success with Ludwig—and Bea's small size. John could hardly consider a dog of merely twenty-two pounds to be a burly adversary, I maintained. "She'll be a breeze to train," I said.

John finally relented, and one chilly evening, in his parka and muffler, he snapped a leash onto Bea's collar. I watched through the kitchen window as John gave our little dog a pep talk, his breath fogging the air. Floodlights shone on our patio and lit it up like a miniature football field.

"Okay, Beatrice," John said, with the determined tone of Ludwig's first instructor. "It's time you learned a few things."

Bea sat in her tripod position, but she wasn't wagging The Bongo. She bent her head back to look up at John and yawned. She stated her feelings plainly: She wanted him to hurry and get to the point because she had important resting to do in her warm basket on this cold night.

John chose to ignore this sign of indifference. "You have to pay attention," he continued. But Bea made no promises. She lay down on her stomach with her front legs out in front of her, a beagle sphinx. Probably thinking that this prone position might be most conducive for success with "Stay," John pressed his palm against her nose and gave the command. Watching him back away to the end of the leash, she shot him a look that said, "What are you talking about?"

When John didn't directly answer, Bea got up and headed toward the front door. "No!" John said, and he pulled her back. With a sideways glance at him, she emphatically contended that this business in the cold had gone on long enough. She wanted to go inside. That very minute.

"You didn't quite get that 'Stay,' did you, Bea?" John asked, frustrated.

"Try 'Come,' " I suggested brightly through the window. "That's the most important thing."

John hauled Bea out to the center of the patio. He fidgeted with his muffler and got ready to resume his role as commander-in-chief of an undisciplined army. He moved away from Bea and took a deep breath. "Come!" he called to his troop.

Bea sat on the bricks without moving. In a resentful tone that edged toward pique, she told him that she was not a mind reader. If he wanted her to do something, he had to make whatever it was clear.

John shook the leash to underscore his request: "Come!" With authority—and displeasure—he tugged Bea toward him. It was like dragging one of the stone lions from the New York City Public Library down the block to 41st Street. Wasn't it enough, Bea stiffly demanded, that she'd sat outside in the cold? And now he was using *force* on her? Was this some prelude to manhandling?

John answered her through gritted teeth: "Come! Now! Immediately!" Vexed, he tugged Bea to her feet.

But Bea would no more come than she would voluntarily skip breakfast. John had met his match. No matter how many times he got Bea to sit and then backed away and called her, she would stiffen her legs against him. "She knows what I want," John shouted to me angrily. "She just won't comply."

When he moved on to "Heel," she jumped and jigged and ran back and forth across the bricks as far as her leash would allow—and barked and yapped her opposition with the silver tongue of William Jennings Bryan. Her arguing was directed not only at John, but also at the gutter downspout, the coiled hose, and the azalea bushes, as if she were trying to get them to take her side. Occasionally, with her ears flapping, she would circle John's legs and, in rebellion, pin them together with her leash. Growing ever more testy, he would untangle himself each time and resume the lesson.

After twenty minutes of this squabbling, he'd had enough. He knew defeat when he saw it, and he didn't want to be out in the cold any more than Bea did. That night she won the argument and persuaded him in no uncertain terms that beagles have wills of their own. From then on, whenever John brought up "Come," "Heel," or "Stay" with her, she would resist with the same resolution and fervor.

I never showed him what I'd found in Thelma Gray's *The Beagle,* which, as you may remember, had shamed me so badly when I began trying to teach Bea to go outside for matters of bathroom hygiene. In talking about obedience training, Ms. Gray brought to our knees those of us with unruly beagles. "The truth is," she said, "the beagle is smart enough to outwit anybody sufficiently dumb enough to let it do it."

◘

I DON'T WANT to leave the impression that all our private conversations with Bea were quibbles and protests. Sometimes, in fact, the discussions were quite the opposite, even beautiful. The most memorable of these, which occurred not long after John and Bea's internecine tiff, marked a radical change in her attitude, and my relationship to her was never the same again.

I had determinedly kept up my attempts to get Bea to sit on my lap in the white wicker rocking chair. And she, with equal determination, had refused to have any part of it. I must have picked her up and tried to hold her three hundred times. But each time, Bea would act as if my lap were a rack or an iron maiden. She insisted that I was being cruel for cornering her in such a torturous fashion, and she would leap to the floor.

Pointing out to her that cuddling could be highly rewarding seemed not to penetrate. Neither did mentioning that I found her indifference to be a stinging personal rebuff. Bea would let me get just so close to her and no closer. Though the Berlin Wall between us had fallen, there was still a sizeable moat with no drawbridge. My Lucy Brown ten-cent psychiatric diagnosis: Bea simply did not yet understand that there was such a thing as love.

I still don't know what went on in her mind to change her. Perhaps she saw me holding a purring Tigger. Maybe one of the more aggressive neighborhood dogs had lunged at the fence and frightened her; instead of telling us about it at the time, she might have stored up the distress and later come to me for comfort. Or maybe she just gradually picked up the mostly loving atmosphere in our house.

There's just no way to be sure about a beagle's mental processes.

Nevertheless, one day I picked her up and expected her to shun me as usual. For a moment, she stood, rigid, on my lap, as if she were about to jump for her life. But then she hesitated. She sat down, a little wobbly at first as she got her balance on my legs. And finally she actually *leaned* against me. Seeming to find no iron maiden, but instead a harbor of security, she pressed her weight against me. I wrapped my arms around her, a cocoon for her chrysalis. And then the floodgates of Bea's love opened.

The finest love there ever was seemed to flow out of her. She told me that she cared deeply about me and that she finally trusted me enough to let me know her feelings. I told her that I would always try my best to live up to them; and, as she nestled her head under my chin, we made sort of a beagle-human pact of endearment.

That moment, for me, was one of pure joy. I like to think that it was the same for Bea. From then on, my lap was her favorite resting place. It turned out that once I'd shown her what love was, she had plenty to teach me about it.

# 5

# Bea's Heritage

Before Bea, I have to admit, I knew nothing about beagles. I'd grown up reading the exploits of Snoopy, and I'd met a few real beagles now and again over the years. But I'd never had more than a passing acquaintance with any of them. At most, my connections had come down to a how-do-you-do and a pat on the head.

With Bea, though, all that quickly changed. Without even realizing it, I became what in the dog world is known as a "beagler," meaning one who befriends or consorts with a member of Bea's breed. And I was "beagling," which originally referred to hunting rabbits or hares on foot with a pack of beagles, but which today can also apply to taking part in any activity with them, including going for walks or tossing Frisbees. With Bea, I was beagling all day long.

Since she'd become such a significant part of my life and I was now wrapped up in beagles, I decided that I owed it to her to learn about her heritage. What I wanted most to know was where Bea had come from in the first place—not specifically from what lab, but, in a broader sense, from what ancestry. How had she gotten to be a speck on the vast landscape of life on earth? What forces had converged for thousands of years to the single point of Bea? If there were a beagle Bible, what would be written in her Book of Genesis?

I checked books out from the library and started reading, and what I often found were obscurities and contradictions. The truth is that Bea's lineage cannot be positively proven, because few records of specific breeds were kept before the recent days of studbooks and dog shows. Breeds are always evolving, so their physical appearance is never the same for long; a medieval beagle may have looked very different from a Victorian one, and this adds to the confusion. Even the name "beagle" didn't appear in English literature until 1475. Before that, small hounds, who could well have been Bea's ancestors, were known as Kennets in one part of England and Veltevers in another—and by altogether different names in France and Italy. You can see why Bea's background is so foggy.

Nobody knows for sure where the name "beagle" came from either. Some speculate that it's derived from the old English *begle,* the French *beigh,* and the Celtic *beag,* for "small," which early beagles probably were. Or the name may be rooted in Old French words for "open wide" and "throat" because beagles are usually so highly verbal, especially when they howl "Aroooooo!" I once heard that "beagle" is from French and Gaelic words for "useless" and "of little value," supposedly because the rabbits and hares that Bea's ancestors hunted were considered unimportant game, compared to, say, deer or boar. (I never told Bea of this early insult to her line.)

Theories conflict about the origin not just of beagles, but of dogs in general: whether they came from the wolf family, or whether they were a separate clan right from the start. Perhaps Bea's Adam and Eve evolved in Asia or Africa in a symbiotic relationship with early humans. The dogs probably trailed prehistoric hunters with hopes they'd leave behind meat scraps; and the hunters may not have chased them away because the dogs could lead them to quarry and howl warnings when dangerous animals lurked in the darkness beyond the campfire. Around 5000 B.C., as hunters settled into villages, so did dogs. Villagers probably tamed and hand-raised pups and started breeding them, and then it was only a matter of time until a beagle appeared on the earth.

Bea's early progenitors may have been bloodhounds

bred with gazehounds, resulting in smaller, faster dogs to track small game. Nobody knows. But around 350 B.C., the Greek historian Xenophon wrote of hunters tracking hares with packs of small hounds. The ancient Romans are thought to have spirited some of those dogs away to Italy after wars with Greece, and they may also have taken them to England. Whether the breed arrived in England in this way or in another fashion, what matters most is that England became the small hounds' natural home, where they evolved and flourished. What a poodle is to Paris, the beagle was to the British countryside.

Mentions of small hounds crop up here and there in early English literature and historical records, and beaglers like to claim that those dogs are early versions of their breed. Pwyll, Prince of Wales during the time of King Arthur, was known to have kept white hounds that might have been Bea's forebears. In the early eleventh century, Canute the Great, king of Denmark and England, decreed a law banishing certain dogs from his royal British forests. He exempted long-eared hounds because they were too small to harm his deer. In the 14th century, Edward III, who was a passionate hunter, brought along 120 hare hounds when he went off to fight France in the Hundred Years' War.

How beagles evolved as a breed separate from other hounds is anyone's guess. Some dog historians speculate that foxhounds or harriers were bred with England's old southern hounds—or even with terriers or spaniels—to create small dogs with champion noses and titanic endurance for chasing game. After these dogs were officially known as beagles, their history becomes easier to follow. Bea's heritage moves from shadows into sunlight, from conjecture to fact. By the 15th century, beagles had become the companions and confidants of royalty. Bea's ancestors have a glittering history of consorting with the upper crust.

England's King Henry VIII may have been a brute to his wives, but he was a muffin toward his beagles. In records of his household, he employed a "Keper of the Begles," whose job was to make sure the dogs were "sweete, wholesome, and cleane." The king once paid three shillings to hire a cart to transport his dogs and spare their paws, and five shillings and sixpence for canvas and nails to make an awning to shield his beagles from sun, wind, and rain.

His daughter, Good Queen Bess, also kept a pack of early Beas, who are depicted in paintings hunting with her royal court or simply sitting loyally beside her. Beagles at that time were so tiny that they were called "glove beagles" because they could fit in a gauntlet, or "pocket beagles" because hunters would carry them around in hunting-coat pockets or saddle panniers. The dogs' barking was so admired that they were also called "singing beagles." Elizabethan beaglers tried to breed Bea's forebears with voices that would harmonize when the dogs howled and yapped on rabbit hunts.

King James I, son of Mary, Queen of Scots (whose loyal dogs stood by her at the scaffold), was probably the most devoted to his beagles of all the royals. He called his wife "deare little beagle" and himself his beagles' "deare dadde." He also referred to his favorite minister, Robert Cecil, Earl of Salisbury, as "my little beagle" because Cecil apparently had a gift for sniffing out subversive political plots. In a letter, the king once mentioned that some of his beagles were "faire," "prettie," and "worthie" enough to sleep on one's bed. Once, just as his ship seemed about to sink during a storm at sea, he was supposed to have shouted, "Save the dogs!"

King George IV was known to have bred what in the 19th century were called "dwarf beagles," tiny lap dogs with long ears, nearly pug noses, and smooth coats (as opposed to the rough, wirehaired coats of other contemporary beagles). The dogs hunted with him regularly, and he even had his portrait painted with them. So did Queen Victoria and Prince Albert, who are portrayed surrounded by tiny, almost white beagles. When Prince Albert would take Bea's ancestors off to hunt in Windsor Great Park, each pack was said to be so carefully matched by height and speed that they could be covered with a single bed sheet as they charged across fields together after a rabbit.

Though Bea's predecessors often found their way into

royal hearts, the common folk in England are thought to have grown indifferent to the dogs. In 1803, the start of a dismal phase in beagle history, the magazine *Sportsman's Cabinet* pointed out that beagles were kept mostly by "rustics" who were too poor to buy a horse and had to hunt on foot, or by sickly gentlemen whose infirmities sapped their stamina and prevented them from more strenuous and exciting hunts on horseback. The *Sportsman's Cabinet* also claimed that the less taxing activity of following a beagle, rather than a faster dog, was considered better for "the feminine gender" and "ladies of the greatest timidity." Beagles sank even farther out of popular favor when fox hunting came into vogue and rabbit-chasing beagles were snubbed.

Because so few people were keeping beagles, they were rarely trotted around the ring in dog shows. In an important show at the Holborn Horse Repository in 1861, out of 240 dogs, only nine beagles were entered. Ten years later, in another show at London's Crystal Palace, the number of competing dogs skyrocketed to 834, but, again, only a measly nine were beagles. Their numbers were similarly paltry at the century's end: in 1892, only twelve packs of beagles and their harrier cousins were listed in a British studbook. Those few dogs may have accounted for much of the stock left at that time in England. The breed might have come close to vanishing.

Fortunately, an antidote to this dreary chapter in Bea's

Book of Genesis was already on its way. In the mid-nineteenth century, the Reverend Philip Honeywood was breeding the dogs and showing his packs of beagles in Essex. I think of Honeywood as like the monks who kept European civilization going by a thread in the Dark Ages when they copied manuscripts that might otherwise have been lost. By breeding beagles, Honeywood maintained their numbers until they regained popularity. His English pack is said to mark the beginning of the modern beagle.

In America, beagles had been hanging around long before Honeywood was born. Supposedly, the dogs had sailed across the Atlantic with Colonial settlers, who needed them to hunt and to guard their homes. In 1642, officials of Ipswich (then known as Aggawam), Massachusetts, ordered every householder whose estate was valued at 100 to 500 pounds to provide a hound or beagle for hunting wolves to protect the town. Later, as life in America got easier and people could concern themselves with things besides warding off wolves, the landed gentry, particularly in the South, hunted foxes and hares on horseback for sport with beagles, who were said to be mostly white and squat, more like dachshunds or bassets.

During the Civil War, Americans had more important things than beagles on their minds, but after Reconstruction, Bea's forebears became prominent again. To perk up their bloodline and breed more attractive dogs, two ardent beaglers, Richard Rowett and Norman Elmore, imported the finest beagles they could find from England: Rosey, Sam, Dolly, Warrior, Ringwood, and Countess. Carefully bred, these dogs were the start of what's said to be the most superior strain of beagles in the United States.

I wanted to believe that Bea was directly descended from them. But either Rowett and Elmore allowed less-than-perfect dogs to have conjugal visits, or Bea came from a completely different line. Her physique differed significantly from the standard for the ideal beagle, drafted by the National Beagle Club of America in 1884 and adopted later that year by the American Kennel Club. This standard of perfection is what judges use at dog shows to rate each entrant, grading the beagle's appearance, bearing, and behavior.

Bea's muzzle, according to the standard, was supposed to be straight and square-cut. But in profile, she had an upturned, ski-jump nose like Richard Nixon's. Her throat should have been "clean and free from folds of skin," but instead, it had the dreaded "dewlap," or sagging neck flesh, that makes judges shudder with horror.

The standard would have labeled Bea's hind legs "cowhocks," or bowlegs. Her back feet splayed out like a duck's. Rather than having straight forelegs, as the standard required, Bea's bent out at the elbows, making her what is disdainfully referred to as "bench-legged," or dachshund-like. Her back, not "short, muscular, and strong," as required, was swayed and bony. Worst of all, she did not always carry her tail "gaily with a slight curve." Certainly after I'd brought her home from the kennel, Bea's tail decidedly drooped.

I know that plenty of admirable people get extremely worked up about this standard and have strong opinions about the perfect beagle. Like Miss America Pageant judges, these beaglers can become highly focused on appearances. But what I tried to tell Bea to keep her from feeling inferior was something along the lines of: Beauty is more than skin-deep, and you can't judge a book by its cover. What's a little dewlap? Or a couple of cowhocks? Superficialities, that's all. If dog-show judges rated beagles on decency and goodness, dusting Bea's trophies would have taken all my time.

□

WHILE I READ all the books about beagles and their history, I kept a list of the most common adjectives used to describe the breed. They were all positive, those deeper-than-skin qualities I'd mentioned. Taken together, the adjectives seemed to me to define another kind of beagle standard—not for physical, but for psychological, even moral, perfection. And, honestly, most beagles live up to it.

In reference after reference, this breed is said to be persevering, determined, hardy, and energetic. That's why all those English kings loved taking beagles on hunts. Beagles are almost invariably described as friendly, affectionate, patient, and loyal—in other words, ideal companions, or "love buckets," as my friend Natalia says. Beagles are also considered courageous, independent, and intelligent. After beagling with Beatrice for a while, I could vouch that all of the adjectives are fair and accurate—not the hyperbole of some besotted beagler—and I had a firsthand understanding of why, out of 150 breeds, beagles are ranked as the fifth most popular in the United States. According to American Kennel Club registration statistics, they are close behind only golden and Labrador retrievers, German shepherds, and dachshunds.

When beagles put all their fine traits into action, they behave in the most exemplary ways. Take, for example, Mini, who'd been abandoned as a tiny pup in the woods of Raleigh, North Carolina. She'd barely survived on her own for three days before Eddie and Patti Clinton discovered her, starving and suffering from parasites, an injured leg, and running sores on her sides. Patti fed her with an eyedropper for weeks and kept her warm on a heating pad until she recovered. As an adult, Mini seemed inclined to return the kindness. When the Clintons' cat gave birth to a kitten with a broken back, for months Mini would snuggle up to him and attend to him like Clara Barton, showering the tiny cat with a beagle's patience and affection.

After Hurricane Fran came along and shook the Clintons' trees like matchsticks, Mini again sprang into action.

In spite of the wind, the Clintons were trying to sleep, but Mini kept whimpering on the porch. The sound wasn't just a quick, quiet "m-m-m-m-m"; it was a humdinger of a whimper—loud, nagging, and unrelenting. Patti climbed out of bed to find out what the dog wanted. At that moment, a tree sliced through their bedroom ceiling. Eddie threw himself on the floor to get out of the way as the trunk crashed onto the bed. The Clintons are certain that Mini had sensed the danger coming and had tried to get them to move to safety. She'd shown a beagle's intelligence.

So did Mollie, who had a bit of dachshund mixed in with her beagle genes. In the ramshackle bungalow where she lived in Hainesport, New Jersey, a kerosene lantern tipped over, and the home went up in flames. Mollie's elderly guardian tried to throw her out the window to safety, but she wriggled out of his hands and began carrying her pups outside one by one. All the while, the fur on her head and back smoldered. Bystanders tried to throw a blanket over her, but she insisted on returning to the burning house again and again. When she finally sat down in the snow with all six of her babies, tufts of burned fur and skin hung from her body. The tip of her nose and the pads of her paws had been burned off, and she held her floppy beagle ears out stiff because they were so painful. Her sacrifice to save her pups said everything about beagles' perseverance and bravery.

Klutz, an elderly mostly-beagle mutt in Lehigh Acres,

Florida, showed these qualities, too, along with colossal loyalty to Lisa Funderburk, his guardian, and Lyndsey, her daughter, who seemed to be Klutz's personal charge. If Lyndsey cried in her crib, Klutz would grab Lisa's pant leg in his teeth and tug her toward her daughter's bedroom. Whenever Lyndsey tried to crawl up the stairs, he'd grab the seat of her coveralls and pull her back to safety.

One day, when three-year-old Lyndsey started heading out the back door, he barked and yapped at her so loudly that Lisa ran to see what was wrong with him. Klutz shrieked and yelped with obvious pain. A rattlesnake was coiled under a bush next to him, ready to strike Lisa's beloved dog a second time.

Klutz collapsed, then got up and staggered toward the snake to keep it away from Lyndsey. As he fell down, the rattler struck him again. And again. With beagle determination, Klutz had refused to give up. He died a hero for his Purple Heart courage.

Of course, not all beagles are tested in such horrendous ways, or asked to climb Mount Everests of sacrifice and giving. Certainly, once Bea came to us, she led a pampered life with no hurricanes, flames, or snakes to threaten her. Still, as time passed, I came to feel that, if needed in a crisis, she'd surely have behaved in just as commendable a fashion as Mini, Mollie, and Klutz. Like those of most of her breed, Bea's eyes constantly seemed to tell me that she'd follow me to the ends of the earth.

Beagles tend to give their all to those they love, and they seem earnest about such "human" ideals as duty and obligation. They are typically indomitable and chipper—with the stiff upper lip of Londoners in the blitzkrieg. They are docile, cheerful, and stalwart when faced with adversity. They're eager to please.

But life with a beagle can also be a challenge because beagles are stubborn; and they have strong opinions about such matters as wanting to sleep on the sofa or take a walk after supper. If they're off leash and get a whiff of something interesting, they press their noses to the ground and go after the scent. No matter how loudly you yell and scream at them, you often cannot distract them or persuade them to return to you. Sometimes when they follow their noses, they can roam for miles and end up lost. They require sturdy fences to keep them from wandering.

These drawbacks of life with a beagle seem small compared to the advantages, however. And with Bea, I became an expert on the advantages. After having her in our house for a year—with puddles or no—we wouldn't have traded her for a winning California lottery ticket. Though I never took to calling John "my deare little beagle," as King James I called his spouse, we came to agree with him that Bea was "faire" and "prettie"—and, certainly, way beyond "worthie."

# 6

# Steps Backward
# and Forward

I'D ALWAYS THOUGHT
that teaching Bea to love would be the key to an idyllic life
with her. Once she opened up and felt confident enough
to care about us, I believed, she would leave behind all her
problems and move on to be a perfect beagle. But, of
course, I was wrong. The ones who'd have it right are the
tribal weavers who purposely make a mistake in an oriental rug because they say that only God is perfect. The
rest of us have to muddle along in life and do the best we
can with our weaknesses and complications.

That's certainly what Bea did, as I discovered late one
Saturday afternoon. While I was doing research at the library, John decided to clean the oven. He stood at the

sink and sloshed soapsuds on the metal rack; and Bea wandered around his feet, as she often did during their private times together in the kitchen. Ludwig was snoring in the bedroom; Tigger was outside patrolling the periwinkle on the lookout for mice. It was an ordinary, meat-and-potatoes kind of day—the kind during which things can take you by surprise.

The rack was unwieldy. As John moved it around to rinse it off, it slipped in his hands and hit the faucet—and metal struck metal with a resounding clang. John thought nothing of it, but then he felt Bea press against his ankle. She was vibrating clear down to her bones.

John set the rack on the counter and bent down to remind her that she was now free from the lab and safe with us. But as he reached to pet her, she seemed to shrivel, then crumble. She staggered toward the refrigerator and sank to the floor. Her head rocked from side to side, and she looked confused—as if a storm were lashing waves inside her skull. In no uncertain terms, she was shouting "Mayday!" For John, it was wrenching to see Bea regress to her days of terror.

He sat down next to her and lifted her into his lap to comfort her, but she continued to sway her head and tremble. He set her down to see if she could walk. She didn't even take a step before she wobbled and her legs gave out. When I came home a few minutes later, that was how I found them—John on the floor holding Bea, whose mind seemed to have left the room. All that remained was a quivering body. "Something's *really* wrong," John said.

He believed that the clang of the rack against the faucet had reminded Bea of a cage door crashing closed; that sound had reactivated all her terrors from the lab and set off a total physical and emotional unraveling. My opinion, on the other hand, was that we were just now seeing the effects of tests or procedures that Bea might have undergone at the lab. If she'd been given an experimental drug, or if her brain had been surgically altered, the effects might have been slow to manifest. Either way, John and I had been wrong to believe that Bea had fully recovered—and it was a devastating realization.

"I'm afraid she's going to die," I said.

"Then we have to face it," John replied.

Andrew agreed to meet us at his clinic, and I held Bea, wrapped in a blanket, while John drove. Rain pinged off the car's roof and added to our gloom. But at least, as Bea nestled against me, she slowly seemed to shake less. In fact, by the time we pulled into the parking lot of the clinic, she wasn't shaking at all. She was back to her old self, eagerly looking out the window at Andrew's row of fire hydrants (his outdoor toilet for his dog patients), and generally acting as if nothing untoward had ever happened to her in her life. In other words, she was making John and me look like alarmists. Now we weren't just worried about her; we were utterly baffled by her behavior.

In the exam room, I kept insisting that Bea really *had* been sick. Andrew checked her eyes, which were no longer glazed, but bright and alert. As John and I searched for prognostications in Andrew's every move, he listened to her heart, took her temperature, palpated her stomach, and rolled back her lips to examine her gums.

Finally, Andrew leaned back against the sink and crossed his feet. "I'm pretty sure Bea had a petit-mal seizure," he said.

"There was nothing petit about it," I said. "It was hugely horrible."

"Could it have anything to do with a noise Bea heard in the kitchen?" John asked. He explained his theory that the oven rack's clang against the faucet had reopened Bea's psychological wounds from the lab.

Andrew agreed that a sudden, loud noise could easily trigger a seizure, especially in a dog with Bea's sensitivity and damaging past. "But there could be a hundred other things that could lead to a seizure," he said. "An infection. A blood chemistry imbalance. Toxins. Genes. Trauma. Stress. A brain tumor."

John and I exchanged anxious glances.

"Don't worry," Andrew said. Bea would have to have many more seizures before we should get concerned, he told us, and if they became frequent, a drug could control them.

Those words helped soothe our worries. We were

even more reassured when we looked at Bea standing on Andrew's steel exam table. Plump and sleek, without a single fearful shiver rippling through her body, she reminded me of a town after a hurricane has swept through—the sun has come out in all its glory, and it seems impossible to believe there were ever such things as wind and rain. Bea held her head high and looked at us with confidence. Her paws were firmly planted on the table's slick metal surface, and her tail wore its sideways smile, as upright and cheerful as anyone could want from a beagle.

Though she was surely not thrilled to be at the clinic, she was behaving with quiet dignity and even courage, in sharp contrast to her first visit to Andrew, when she had cowered, trembled, urinated, and rolled into a ball to protect herself. Then she had expected cruelty and suffering, and she hadn't had the vaguest notion that life could be good. Now, if beagles could sing, she'd be letting us know that the corn was as high as an elephant's eye. She was both chipper and commanding.

Full of pride in Bea, I remembered my friend Wendy Shelton's standard rule for recovery. She had been a veterinarian at the University of California at Davis, where Woofer, Ludwig's mother, had been hospitalized for a month with systemic lupus. Because Woofer still couldn't walk when the time came to bring her home, John and I, with heavy hearts, had rolled her on a gurney to our car.

Wendy followed, carrying plastic bags of Woofer's medicine. She explained that healing was just like life: You take a step forward and a step back, and then maybe two forward and one back, and three forward and three back. There are ups and downs, she said, but you hope the general trend is up. You have to climb on the seesaw and ride out the process.

That's exactly what Woofer did. In the beginning, she couldn't struggle to her feet; she would just lie there, her face depressed and dark. But then sometimes she would manage to stand; and I would loop a bath towel under her belly and support her for a few hesitant steps before she lay down gloomily again. After a week, she'd occasionally limp around on her own. Eventually, she was hobbling on bad days and walking on good ones, and, finally, one afternoon she pranced, full of life, on sturdy legs across the kitchen.

I saw this same phenomenon of recovery in Bea. Since she'd come to us, she'd muddled along and taken psychological forward and backward

*Woofer sunning on the deck*

steps that paralleled Woofer's physical ones while she'd healed. Just an hour earlier, Bea had seemed to slide back by buckling under her sensitivity and having a seizure. But now she'd also moved ahead, apparently learned to work around her fears, and refused to be intimidated by a man in a white lab coat.

Bea may have regressed that day, but she also advanced. She was making do in spite of being vulnerable, and in her mental rearview mirror, her trauma from the lab seemed to have receded from a mountain to a speck. I don't know if she managed this through force of will or by somehow gaining new perspective. But any way you looked at her, she was a phoenix rising from the ash-heap of her past.

BECAUSE OF BEA, I thought a lot about vulnerability and sliding now and again into what may seem like an abyss. I could understand her because I'd had to learn to live with my own sensitivities, and certainly I'd taken my share of life's backward steps. But Bea helped me see that those steps, rather than being permanent disasters, can sometimes lead to important gifts wrapped humbly in newspaper and twine. They'd prodded me along in a positive direction or forced me into crucial insights that were far more than just silver linings to my clouds.

Before I went to the university, for example, I had absolutely no idea what I wanted to do with my life. My parents regularly hinted around that it was time for me to chose a direction for myself and find a "bent," as my mother put it. But though I was interested in almost everything, there was no single subject for which I felt a driving passion. All that changed, though, when I signed up for an introductory biology course in my freshman year.

The professor started our very first lecture with the words, "In the beginning there was hydrogen gas." After that, he led us through evolutionary theory, touching upon photosynthesis, the Krebs cycle, and the double helix. I was mesmerized. I had always loved plants, oceans, stars — actually, anything in nature — and especially birds and other animals. Certain that I could find no field more fitting to me than biology, I joyfully declared that subject as my major. Some day I would study wolves or herons in the wilderness, I told myself. At last my life was set on course. I would navigate by fur and feathers.

In my English class that same semester, I had learned the ancient Greek maxim "Know thyself." I should have known myself well enough to see what lay ahead. In our biology lab syllabus were assignments for dissecting a prenatal pig; and when it came to animals, I had always been what my friend Kim's ex-husband called her: an exposed nerve-ending. Show me an animal suffering in any way, and my emotions would surge from discomfort to anguish. I once heard that a surgical drainage tube had been put into my dog, and, without even seeing the dog or the tube, I fainted and toppled off my chair.

Born on St. Francis's feast day, I'd probably had this sensitivity to animals since my zygote days; it may have been an inherited trait from my father, a supremely gentle symphony conductor and composer, who once left the room weeping when he saw a dog about to die in a TV movie. As early as age three, I wailed inconsolably in westerns when Roy Rogers jabbed his spurs into Trigger's sides, and I never even made it through *Bambi*. Sitting in a ribbed felt chair at the Varsity Theater and watching the animals running for their lives from the forest fire, I cried so hard that my parents had to take me home.

When I got older, I also cried over trout my grandfather caught and put in a bucket of water that turned red from the fish's just-hooked mouths. To shut me up, my mother told me that fish had no nerves and couldn't feel pain. "Get tough!" she said to me, as she did for years.

What better way to learn about the nerves of fish than by studying biology? And how better to show how tough I could be than by dissecting that prenatal pig? I was determined that my sensitivities would not win out this time, and I steeled myself as my lab partner, Tommy Richardson, and I walked up to a pile of small bodies stacked up like pastries on a platter.

Recoiling, I told myself that our baby pig had never been born and, therefore, had never known pain. Regardless, my steel resolve splintered into tiny pieces, then melted to mush. I could not bring myself even to touch the pig, so Tommy did the cutting and the probing of her tissues, veins, and organs, while I averted my eyes. When I left the lab, I was sweaty and nauseated—and not just because of the sickening smell of formaldehyde. I had to admit to myself that there was no way on earth I could ever be a biologist. I endlessly berated myself: I was a failure, crushed, lost.

In the next year, still smarting from defeat, I changed my major to math and then finally to English. Reading *Middlemarch* seemed far more benign than dissecting pigs and far more interesting than chasing imaginary numbers. Because my father had always urged me to be a college teacher, I went to graduate school and then took a job in the English Department at the University of Hawaii. By then, years had passed since my crashing disappointment about biology; yet I still occasionally asked myself if I'd given up my dream too easily. With determination and maturity, could I have grown a tough hide after all?

One day, during my first summer in Hawaii, I was scribbling the assignment for my writing class on the blackboard when I suddenly became aware of dogs howling on the roof of an adjacent building. These were lonely, wretched, desperate cries I was hearing; they were imbued with misery. Shaken, I slammed the windows shut. After class I went to the department chairman to find out what was wrong with the dogs.

They were experimental animals, he told me, probably being used in biology or physiology labs. "I know how you feel," he said. "The dogs upset me, too. But there's nothing to be done about it."

In those days, the authority of administrators loomed large in my mind. It never occurred to me that I could have marched over to the lab director, asked why the dogs were so disconsolate, and suggested that they either be treated kindly or freed forever from their life in cages. I could even have threatened to organize a protest if available alternatives for research were not used instead of the dogs, or if experiments on them were not guaranteed to be pain-free and intended solely to save lives. Instead, for that whole summer I kept the classroom windows closed. My sympathetic students seemed not to mind the sweltering. We grimly endured the muffled howls that penetrated the glass, and we forged ahead in that inferno of a room.

But with each cringe at the howls and each rivulet of sweat down my back from the heat, I thanked God for my sensitivity. As a university freshman, it may have caused me grief and shame over what I'd thought then was abject failure, but it had also protected me from a career dead-end, where I'd have been like a cactus trying to make a go of it in a rainforest. Vulnerabilities and all, I was glad to be me.

◘

AFTER BEING SO BRAVE at Andrew's clinic, Bea truly jumped a psychological hurdle. She seemed to take on a new identity, like Cinderella sliding her foot into the glass slipper as a scullery maid and being instantly transformed into a princess. A vet technician, in fact, once called Bea "The Princess" because, she said, Bea always expected to have her needs met immediately and lovingly — a day-and-night contrast to her early bedraggled-urchin era. Wherever Bea went now, she carried herself with a new self-assurance.

Occasionally, however, she did have a seizure. It always seemed to be set off by something that startled her, and usually that something was a loud noise, just like the metal clang. Her longest, most intense seizures always occurred when an unfamiliar sound, such as fireworks or carpenters' hammering, jolted her out of a deep sleep. Not yet awake enough to get her bearings in the present and remember that she was now secure, she would wobble to us, and we would hold her until the seizure passed — and she returned to her exuberance.

These incidents were never frequent enough for Bea to need medication, but each one made us wonder if she was suffering from a dog's version of the flashbacks humans can suffer after trauma. Instead of mental images of hand grenades blasting around a foxhole, she might have simply felt a vague but overpowering sense of fear. We'd never know. John and I did always feel, though, that her seizures were the last remaining vestige of her former terror, the part imbedded too far inside her for us to reach and help her conquer. That was something she would have to live with, by herself. We could only try to comfort her.

As hard as her seizures were to witness, they did make very apparent to us the intensity and depth of what Bea had overcome, and they showed starkly her admirable courage. They also made all the more remarkable her new poise—and even her beagle optimism, which, we believed, cloaked her sensitivity and probably made it easier to bear. We learned to live with the seizures without being afraid. They were just momentary setbacks, we believed—short timeouts after which our beagle would again be Bea.

# 7

# A Confident Beagle

Aт LONG LAST, WE HAD a self-assured beagle. One of the most overt signs of the metamorphosis was her sudden interest in people. Formerly terrified of strangers and rather standoffish with guests in our house, Bea began to relate in a very cordial manner to whoever happened to be around. With the confidence of a model swishing her taffeta skirt on a Paris runway, Bea would enter a room and present herself for petting and attention — as if it were her due.

In a gentle, quiet way, Bea became quite social, and she made many friends, one of whom was our houseguest Sharon, a tough and intimidating Russian lawyer. With just one arch of her eyebrow, Sharon could have withered a Moscow mafia thug, but Bea got only tenderness from her. Sharon would sit for hours on the sofa, cooing baby talk to Bea, who would put her paws on Sharon's knees in a position of rapt attention. Russian attorneys, she told Sharon, were the only people alive worthy of notice. When Sharon returned to St. Petersburg, she was so taken with Bea that she got herself a dog.

Our neighbor Jean, a kindly, proper English lady, related to Bea as Brit to Brit—tally-ho and all that. At our Easter lunch one year, as Bea was making the rounds of our guests and working the room, she stopped to say hello to Jean, who affectionately patted her head. "Love just pours out of this dear little doggy," Jean said. "She takes it for granted that her love will be returned." Bea nosed Jean's hand to ask for more and reminded me of the not-so-distant past when she'd shrunk even from the friendliest hands.

My friend and writing mentor Martha also adored Bea. One night, after dinner at a Chinese restaurant, I let Bea out of the car for an evening sniff in the parking lot. She immediately affixed herself to Martha's feet. "Aren't you just the sweetest?!" Martha murmured. "Hasn't this little angel become the friendly one?" Yes, Bea had.

Seeing her so confident was a pleasure, but sometimes her self-assurance could fall into the category of too much of a good thing. I don't want to give the impression that

Bea became arrogant, but she could on occasion seem a little too full of herself for our taste. We first discovered this on a routine visit to Andrew for her rabies shot.

Andrew politely pointed out to us that Bea had dragon breath, and its source was her teeth. If plaque continued to build up between her gums and enamel, infections could follow—and Bea, he warned, could even end up with no teeth at all. Brushing them was the best insurance against this kind of dental future.

"You've got to be kidding," John said. "Bea would never let us near her with a toothbrush."

"I'll bet she would," Andrew countered. He handed us a white toothbrush and a bottle of a thick blue solution that looked like it belonged in a beaker on a Bunsen burner. We should open Bea's mouth and "go to it," he said, every day or two for the rest of Bea's life.

As I took the brush and solution from Andrew, I knew how Sisyphus felt the first time he said hello to his rock. "Are you *sure* we have to do this?" I asked.

"It would help," Andrew answered.

On the ride home, Bea sat on my lap and watched passing cars. John and I were silent. At lunch, we talked about the weather forecast. We did not discuss The Dreaded Act that lay ahead. At dinner, we discussed the rain gurgling down our drainpipes in torrents. John wondered if he should check to see if leaves were plugging up the gutters. We decided not. We did not mention beagle teeth.

We washed the dishes, and, as Bea slept in the kitchen, I began to re-read *Great Expectations* while John thumbed through the *Wall Street Journal.* Then, at 10:30, I decided we could no longer stay mired in avoidance.

"Don't you think we'd better get out the brush?" I asked John.

He clearly wanted to escape his duty to Bea's teeth. Without a word, he folded his newspaper, went to the bathroom, and brushed his own. When he returned and pulled back the covers to climb into bed, the subtle pressure of my question finally got to him. "I don't want to do it," he said.

"We can't let Bea's teeth rot," I said. "You do what you have to do in life, and we're being asked to brush our beagle's teeth."

"Where would we do it?" John was weakening.

"In the downstairs bathroom she won't be able to grip the tile counter with her toenails and escape."

John squeezed his eyes closed for a moment, clearly trying to blot beagle teeth from his mind, then headed toward the kitchen. He was shuffling his corduroy slippers more than usual, I noticed. In her wicker basket, Bea looked smaller and more vulnerable than she had in many months. She was curled up, her legs tucked under her, and she looked at us with eyes of heart-tugging innocence.

"Grab her," I said.

"*You* grab her," John said. "You're the one who wants to do it."

Bea may not have fully understood the antecedent of "it," but she did sense our apprehension. She got up from her bed and shook her body as if trying to get rid of bath water. Then she planted her legs in front of her, like short, tilted STOP signs, and told us that she didn't know exactly what we had in mind; but we were acting peculiar, and she didn't trust us. Not one bit.

John worked his fingers around her collar and started marching her toward the stairs. In protest she bolted, leapt, skidded around the kitchen, threw herself at cabinets, and told us plainly that she was not going anywhere. Chasing her was like trying to catch a thickly buttered alligator. Nevertheless, John finally managed to pick up Bea. In grim silence, I got the toothbrush and blue solution, and we filed downstairs.

The bathroom walls looked prison green; the mirror, dark. Bea eyed us, looking shifty. As John set her on the counter, I held the toothbrush out to him.

"You have smaller hands," he protested.

Accepting my fate as the appointed brute, I poured blue solution on the toothbrush and aimed it at Bea's mouth. She immediately clamped her jaws shut; and she bit down even harder as John worked his fingers between her lips and started prying. When he tried to wriggle his

thumbnail between her teeth to start at least a crack between her uppers and lowers, his nail bent like a rubber
spear against her fortress of enamel.

The time had come for drastic measures. I set the
toothbrush down in front of Bea, so she could get used to
the sight of it, and I went to the kitchen for her box of
b-i-s-c-u-i-t-s. I rattled the box for dramatic effect, then set
it beside her—a promise of ecstasy to come if she cooper-
ated. As Bea eagerly nosed the box, I caught her off-guard
and rammed the brush into her mouth. She chomped
down like a vise on the plastic. I tried to jiggle the handle
to get her to open her mouth enough for me to brush, but
she would have none of it. "Come on, Bea," I pleaded.

We were dreaming, Bea told us forthrightly, if we
thought she would go along with us. The toothbrush stuck
out of her mouth at a jaunty angle. Blue-tinged saliva drib-
bled from her lips and splattered on the counter, like a
Jackson Pollock painting. I raised Bea's muzzle toward me
but managed only a few ineffectual swipes at her teeth before she began to chew the brush. If she couldn't have a
biscuit, she explained, she was going to make do with bristles and plastic. When I finally got the brush away from
her, she puckered her lips and, with a pent-up *p-tooey*, spit
blue all over the mirror.

There was no question that we were trying to carry
out an impossible task. As far as John was concerned,

Bea's teeth were going to have to rot. But I was thrilled that she felt confident enough to be assertive. Instead of our brushing her teeth, Andrew could clean them now and again, after all.

◘

FOR BEA, standing up to John and me, who loved her, was one thing, but taking on an opponent who'd like to see her dead was quite another. Nevertheless, this is just what she did.

One night, long after John and I had gone to bed, she suddenly let out a piercing, eardrum-vibrating yowl. She broke through the cardboard barrier we had erected to corral her in the kitchen and raced downstairs to the basement, followed closely by Ludwig. Jangled out of a peaceful sleep, John and I staggered after the dogs. We found Bea at the bottom of the stairs, rearing on her hind legs, howling, and yapping as if she'd lost her mind. A shocked raccoon was clinging to the laundry-room ceiling, wildly pedaling her back feet.

The raccoon was fluffy and sumptuous. Davy Crockett would have taken one look at her and thought of caps and stew. Her black eyes shone with defiance. We could touch her, she warned; but we'd end our lives as ribbons.

With her barks, Bea threatened ribbons back—ribbons sliced into confetti. I'd never have believed that she could be whipped up into such a frenzy if I hadn't seen it with my own eyes. In case the raccoon decided to come down from the wall and show Bea a thing or two, I grabbed Bea's collar and tugged her, still snarling, up the stairs; and John followed, dragging Ludwig. With their quarry "treed" in the laundry room, they were desperate to finish off their hunt with teeth in flesh.

Back downstairs, we found the raccoon still hanging from the molding. She'd gotten into the house through the exterior basement door, then sneaked over to the storage area, torn the cover off the kibble vat, and scattered Science Diet all over the floor. We were not so dumb as to try and shoo her out, but we did snap the rubber lid back on the kibble with hopes she'd leave without stopping for a second round of gluttony. More important, we hoped she'd never return and invite another beagle ambush.

All night, in her newfound hunter's mode, Bea barked like a psychotic—and John mumbled, to no one in particular, "How come we never get any peace and quiet in this house?" The next morning the raccoon had disappeared, and John locked the basement door to keep her from another soiree with our kibble. But over breakfast, I glanced out to the deck, and in my peripheral vision, I saw something gray and black and fat. It was the raccoon, sitting on the rail and flicking her ringed tail below her plump haunches. Through the window she glowered, scolded, menaced—and put us on notice that she was preparing to turn us into hamburger.

Bea lunged at the window. When the raccoon wisely left to bivouac on the higher ground of a redwood tree, Bea ran back to the heater register in the living room, where she and Ludwig had yapped all morning. She now egged him on for another barking fest. When John put his ear against the register, he heard tiny, pianissimo squeaks. The raccoon on our deck railing was the mother of babies, who were nesting somewhere in our house and hungry for breakfast. The locked basement door was preventing her from getting to them.

John and I searched for the raccoon nest in every cobwebbed cranny of the basement, with no success. We finally gave up and left the door open, so the mother could come and go at leisure in our new raccoon hotel; and I went to the Humane Society for a have-a-heart trap. I intended to ensnare the mother and then have an animal-control officer take her and the babies to a wildlife rehabilitation center, where they would live until they could be released together as a family in a woods. The plan seemed foolproof. But foolproof plans can melt in the fire of overwhelming obstacles, and my obstacle was that I was dealing with the Einstein of raccoons.

Day after day, I put peanut butter at the back of the cage, set the latch, and left my lure, like a small, wire Trojan horse, just outside the basement door. Day after day, the mother would feast without stepping on the metal plate that would close the cage behind her. And day after day, Bea snapped her teeth and howled, a hunter on the rampage, until even Ludwig seemed to grow sick of her.

I lectured Bea repeatedly about the importance of silence, especially when John and I were trying to sleep, but she just wouldn't listen. The Muhammad Ali in her had taken over, and I could not get her to sit down for an honest dialogue about her pugilism problem. Meanwhile, the raccoon finished up the first jar of peanut butter, and then I bought a second, economy-size. When that was gone, I upped the bait to chicken and kibble—and she continued dining alfresco at our café.

Tensions in our house were mounting, and Bea was beside herself—until around midnight a week later, when I heard a metal snap, then desperate clattering that unleashed still more beagle yowls. Under our flashlight's beam, the mother bristled her whiskers, bared her teeth, and clawed the wire of the cage in which she was now trapped. But her belligerence seemed not to intimidate the animal-control officer who arrived around 2:00 A.M. He hauled the caged mother to his truck, then ripped out one of our basement walls with a crowbar to remove the raccoon babies.

Once the family was gone, I'm relieved to say, Bea finally resumed her role as our gentle companion. But now we knew about her secret dark streak of aggression. Maybe I was rationalizing, but personally I was glad that Bea's years in a lab hadn't squelched her hunting instincts. I kept telling John that Bea had been defending what she'd clearly come to believe was *her* house and family. There was a lot to be said for having a confident guard-dog around.

John argued that Ludwig was already doing a fine job guarding us, and that Bea's protection was redundant. It took him a long time to forgive her — approximately the week it took him to catch up on his sleep.

□

AFTER BEA HAD LIVED with us for several years, we bought a slightly ramshackle, old adobe house in a rural area south of San Francisco, not far from where John worked. The house had massive, rough-hewn redwood doors and ceiling beams. It reminded us of a miniature California mission. Best of all, it was surrounded by a redwood forest and a fenced acre of backyard for Bea, Tigger, and Ludwig. We were relieved to have found such an interesting house, but, at the same time, we worried about Bea's reaction to losing the only home she'd ever known.

John and I discussed what "home" might mean to her. Was it the actual house we were about to leave? Or was it simply the two of us, who had worked so hard to make her feel secure? We couldn't know the answer. Nor could we know if Bea would lose her moorings and regress, or if she'd sail into the new house with confidence. That was the question mark on our horizon.

Certainly, Bea's attitude toward the movers reflected no lack of self-assurance. Locked up in the study with Ludwig and Tigger, she barked ferociously and announced that excised flesh was the least of what could happen if they didn't turn and run. She was willing and able to carry out the mother of all attacks, and the men had better not forget it.

For two days, as the men packed up our belongings, I was an envoy, negotiating peace between Bea and the movers and keeping her out of their way. Then they hauled off our possessions, and I let Bea free in the empty house. Together, we walked around to say good-bye to all that was so familiar—the gate John had built to keep Ludwig from running the streets, the persimmon tree we'd watched grow from a stick to a leafy, fruitful member of the family, the deck railing that Tigger had jumped on so many times she'd worn it down, the bedroom window where I liked to sit and ponder. I kept telling myself that a new life was waiting, but I was sad to relinquish the old one. I was grateful that the animals would be coming along as keepers of our history and ties to our happy memories.

Once at the new house, Bea certainly did not share my sadness or nostalgia. She pranced in as if she owned the place, explored each room, and studied the smells and

secrets of former occu-
pants. With her nose to
the floor, she crossed each
room from corner to cor-
ner. Then she checked all
the perimeters for infor-
mation buried between
the walls and the carpet's
edge, and finally she just
moseyed around at ran-
dom. In only an hour, she
knew far more about the
house than John, I, or

*Tigger*

Ludwig—or Tigger, who was hiding, spooked, in a corner
of the bathroom.

Ludwig, hanging back with considerable reserve, did
not condescend to look around. He lay in the middle of the
living room, frowned at us, and demanded to know the
hour of our departure for home. He recognized our furni-
ture, but what the devil was it doing here? And why had
I just fed him dinner on the kind of paper plate used only
by peasants?

Bea, it turned out, was the only one of us who took all
the upheaval in stride. Actually, she chose that night to ad-
vance another giant step forward. As John and I ate the
picnic supper that our former neighbor Jean, Bea's British

friend, had packed for us, Bea walked to the back door and pressed her nose to the glass.

"Grrrrmmmm." The clearing of a beagle throat. "Grrrrrrmmmmmmm. Grrrrrrrrrmmmmmmmmmmmmmmmmm."

John and I exchanged knowing looks. Surely, Bea wasn't asking for the first time in her life to be let out. But, indeed, she was. She politely "grrmmed" until I got up and opened the door for her; then she dashed out to the patio and sniffed her way up a few steps to the redwood grove. She circled around, as if she was becoming acquainted with the terrain and finding a congenial spot—and then she squatted.

Her puddle was a miracle to John and me. We felt as if birds in the redwoods were singing *Un Bel Di* and stars were shooting like Roman candles through the heavens. We hugged Bea, praised her for her enlightenment, and gave her congratulatory bites of Jean's quiche since we had no hotdogs. We called her Boogle, Woogle, and Beepsie Boop, and we told her that three years of hygienic barbarity had been a short time, really, and we'd always known she'd come around. Bea's elevator had finally gone all the way up. Not once did she ever commit an indelicacy in the house again.

◘

IN THE NEXT MONTHS we unpacked, and I got back to work. Though I was still not yet secure as a freelance

writer, I'd been slowly establishing myself in my new career. Starting with art reviews for a weekly newspaper,
I'd worked my way up to feature articles for women's,
business, and in-flight magazines. I nearly always had
enough assignments to keep me at my desk every day for
long hours. Though I was grateful for the work, I would
often look out my office window and long to be in the
beauty of nature.

In February, great blue herons that made me think of
pterodactyls arrived for their annual roosting in a redwood grove next door. They would fold up their legs like
collapsible yardsticks in order to sun themselves in our
trees. Their looming presence never seemed to bother the
small birds who came to the feeder outside my window.
My most regular customers were blue jays, towhees,
finches, and doves. Deer also stopped by, along with
squirrels, raccoons, rabbits, and an extremely furtive bob-
cat. Bea, ever combat-ready, would howl and bark with all
her might at these interlopers. During interviews for articles I wrote, I would often have to lock her up in another
room to keep her from drowning out the quotes I was
recording.

In April, ferns sent up new swords to herald spring.
Blossoms exploded pink on our plum tree, and soft gray
catkins appeared on our pussy willow. Daffodils surprised
me by inching from the ground and adding yellow brush-
strokes to the picture out my window. Azaleas and rho-

dodendrons joined in with swatches of pink, white, and purple.

Bea, too, seemed to get into the spirit of spring and beginning anew, and potential that had been dormant in her all her life started to emerge. She began to take longer and longer forays outdoors and learned how to go off on her own and find her way back. Every day, with great concentration, she would prowl the fenced part of the forest behind our house.

From my desk, I could see her, consumed by her newly discovered tracking instincts, pick up a real or imaginary scent of rabbit. She would jump up on her back legs and howl "Arroooo!" to announce "You're doomed" to all small local animals and send them scampering to Los Angeles. Then she would charge through the ferns and circle the trees with her nose skimming the ground. Or she would take the forest by zigzag, running back and forth in diagonals, as if she were forging a path of giant rickrack. That way, no matter where her quarry might have run, she could find its trail and press on.

Unlike her nearly hysterical barks at the mother raccoon and the movers, the howls and yaps I heard from Bea on her forest expeditions were throaty, raucous, and filled with hope and expectation. As she ran through the thickest underbrush, the only visible sign of her would be the white tip of her tail. She might well have been running over dales with her English relatives, I thought. Transformed by freedom, Bea was finally living her true nature and doing what her breed was always meant to do. She was a beagle at her very best.

# 8

# The Battle of
# Bea's Bulge

Y OU'D HAVE THOUGHT
that Bea's running around in the forest would have kept
her svelte. Actually, though, after a few years in our new
house, she weighed thirty-five pounds, which made her
quite portly. Her candidacy for Jenny Craig, I learned, is
supposedly a common problem for beagles—and possibly
even a genetic inclination. I once read that the tendency toward corpulence might have evolved because Bea's early
ancestors often hunted—and ate—with Irish wolfhounds.
During meals, the beagles may have tried to match the
gorging of the larger dogs, and those beagles' descendents
are predisposed toward the same overeating. Who knows?

What John and I did know was that one primary

cause of Bea's bulk, besides possibly her genes, was her propensity toward sloth. After her initial exuberance over forays in the redwoods, she began to spend more and more time lounging around and sleeping. She had become a rampant hedonist. As I toiled diligently at my desk, she, in sharp contrast, seemed not to have the slightest notion of the Calvinistic virtues of discipline and effort. With her life centered on self-indulgence, she mastered the art of repose.

During the day, she would assume a variety of sleeping positions. She would start the morning flopped on her stomach with her front legs stretched out beyond her muzzle and her rear legs extended along each side of her tail — so she looked like a chubby ear of corn. By 10:00, she'd roll onto her side and push her legs out, with her body in an extremely rounded "C." By noon she'd curl into a ball the shape of a kidney bean and tuck her nose against her ample belly. In the afternoons, Bea would lie, limp, on her back, with her legs flopped out on both sides. Or she'd languidly walk to her

*The rampant hedonist*

bed and sink into it, looking as if she'd just been poured onto her pillow, her ears floating on the denim.

Accompanying these napping postures were snores that varied with the intensity of her sleep: If she were merely dozing, her breaths made the scraping sounds of branches against a window, but a deeper sleep brought muffled rumbles, like landslides in a deep cave. As she was about to wake for supper, her breaths would get shallow again, possibly in joyful anticipation of food. From the sides of her mouth, she would squeak snores that made me think of fingers rubbing a balloon. All this lolling and snoring burned few calories, so when Bea *did* get up, she tottered, an ungainly little blimp.

John and I were partly to blame for Bea's plumpness. Sure, twice a day we very responsibly tried to feed her a proper portion of meat and kibble, and we genuinely intended not to give her too many biscuits. Nevertheless, wanting to show her we loved her and make up for her early years of deprivation, we were guilty of slipping extra spoonfuls of food into her bowl, and her consumption of Milk-Bones reached a box a week.

We also succumbed far too often to Bea's begging. At supper each night, with the most heart-wrenching pathos, she would express the desperation of a beagle fighting for her life during the Irish potato famine. She would station herself near our feet and stare at our plates, her eyes following our forks as if their every movement determined her survival. At the smell of something she really liked, such as cheese or bread, she would hang a quarter of her pink tongue from her mouth, glinting with a droplet of expectant drool. She'd smack her lips and rock on her front legs to remind us that she was still there . . . waiting.

If we ignored her, she would pant, bristle her eyebrows, and whimper the nearly silent squeaks of a beagle in the throes of death. She'd droop her eyes and look at us with the mournful expression of a starving-Armenian beagle. Sometimes her eyes would actually water from the pain of her hunger, and she would cock her head with pleading and despair. If that didn't work, she'd pace around the table for a better view of what we were eating, or she'd put her paws on our knees, fix her eyes on us, and ask how we could ever be so niggardly as not to set our plates on the floor and give her our entire supper.

In the face of these persuasive tactics, John and I were helpless. Steamrollered, we'd slip her a bit of this or that, and then, of course, she'd immediately look up at us again like Oliver Twist, beseeching in a small, thin voice, *"Please,* can't I have more porridge?" Over the years Bea's "porridge" added up, and the sum was pudge.

Clearly, she needed to get her mind off food and do something besides nap. I decided that one way to accomplish this might be to find her a purpose in life besides eating, and a meaningful reason to get out of bed every day. I'd read about fulfilling jobs for beagles, and I wondered if I could convince Bea to take one. Though my skills of persuasion couldn't begin to compare with hers, I considered laying out her employment options and trying to prod her into some kind of slimming career.

I knew I would never attempt to talk her into joining a hunter's beagle pack, which might require whole days of running. Though Bea would become muscular and lean, she simply wasn't up to such exertion. But she had the potential to be a splendid therapy dog, I believed, since she could easily coax smiles from discouraged senior citizens in convalescent hospitals or give disturbed children some of the love they may have missed in life. She would also have been a good hearing dog. At the sound of a telephone or smoke alarm, she could run to alert a deaf person and perhaps even save a life. If she were to work either job, she might shed pounds while helping others.

If altruism weren't enough to motivate Bea, perhaps fame would be a stronger temptation. She could become an actress and experience the thrill of trotting onstage to receive an Oscar or Emmy. At the very least, she could watch herself on-screen, and that would be exciting even if all she did was a TV commercial. A director's dream, Bea wouldn't need training in the Stanislavsky method to convey the ecstasy of Alpo. If she made herself available, Hollywood agents would swarm after her, I was sure, but she'd have to make a sacrifice. Only beagle sylphs got the glamorous roles.

Bea might also consider the moral obligation of putting one's gifts to use for the betterment of mankind. Without question, she had received one grace in life that towered above all her others: her extraordinary sniffer. When it came to noses, she was a noble and I was a serf. I pick up odors with a paltry five million scent receptors in my nasal passages, whereas a beagle is blessed with about 220 million—allowing Bea not merely to detect the faintest of scents, but also to distinguish between them. And the part of her brain that receives messages from her nose's nerves was much more highly developed than mine; she was able to store huge amounts of information about smells there and do special work that would allow her to contribute to society in ways that I, a nasal underling, never could.

Bea could join the United States Department of Agriculture's Beagle Brigade as a detector dog, for instance. Wearing a spiffy green jacket inscribed with the words "Protecting America's Agriculture," Bea would act like a small, portable X ray machine—but using her nose to investigate suitcases in an airport's baggage-claim and passenger-arrival areas. If she noticed mangos, apples, beef, pork, or other forbidden foods tucked illegally inside, she would be asked to inform her handler—a cinch of a job. Though she would have to get used to being denied the delicious foods that she discovered, she could have the satisfaction of stopping troubles that could destroy the nation's food supply: fruit canker, hog cholera, hoof-and-mouth disease, and swine fever, for instance. Had a beagle been on the scene in 1980, a few sniffs might even have discovered the one measly orange that's believed to have brought the Mediterranean fruit fly into California in 1980 and cost $100 million to eradicate.

If airports turned out not to be Bea's thing, she could use her exquisite nose to find termites, ants, and powder-post beetles in homes and commercial buildings. Of course, she'd need to get her weight down enough to wriggle into cramped areas that only a trim beagle could reach, such as dark crawl-spaces and the inches between walls, under decks, and around floorboards and joists. Then, when told, "Show me," she'd be expected to howl and paw wherever any wood-boring insects happened to have set up shop. If Bea were like most beagles on this job, she'd do a great service to property owners by spotting as few as twenty of the pests—a phenomenal display of nasal supremacy.

The more I thought about bringing up potential jobs like this to Bea, though, the more I came to see that neither service nor noblesse oblige were high on her list of priorities. She just wasn't the type of dog who felt she had to save the world, and she was a glutton for food, not for the adulation of talent scouts or the Department of Agriculture. Gainful employment was not so crucial for her as it had always been for me, and I knew I shouldn't try to force my values on her. Besides, in the end, I selfishly wanted Bea to stay with me while I worked alone in my office all day. Though being my companion wouldn't take inches off her waistline, at least the job was respectable, and she was extremely qualified for it.

◘

JOHN AND I DENIED the severity of Bea's portliness until a discovery forced us to face facts. One night, as we started dinner and she began the prologue of her nightly drama for handouts, I patted her with hopes that affection could compensate for the morsels we were denying her. On one of Bea's sides, I felt a soft, squishy lump, slightly larger than a lemon. With alarm, I asked John to take a look.

He explored the lump with his fingertips. To compare it with her other side, he probed there, too—and found another lump. Because of Bea's seizures, we'd become especially aware of possible lingering effects from the lab, and now we were immediately concerned that she might have been slowly growing tumors induced by an experiment. Though we tried to reassure each other that matching tumors on both sides of her body were highly unlikely, I took her to Andrew to make sure.

He gave Bea a quick judgmental look and declared the lumps to be fat pads. "You really need to put her on a diet," he said. To emphasize his point, he listed potential hazards that might accompany a dog's obesity: lung, heart, and liver disease, for instance, or a propensity for disk problems and arthritis. If Bea ever needed surgery, her fat could bring on complications.

Clearly, I did not want these risks casting shadows on Bea's health. So at each meal, according to Andrew's prescription, I began to feed her only a small spoonful of high-fiber canned food and a carefully measured half-cup of special, low-cal kibble. I took her for two brisk walks a day, even if I had to drag her outside into the rain. No matter how convincingly she pleaded about her wish to stay dry and her need for a snack, I did not relent. Biscuits were strictly forbidden. When she begged, I turned my back on her and tossed words like "discipline" and "self-control" over my shoulder.

For some moderation during this Spartan regime, I did feed Bea, at Andrew's suggestion, lettuce, carrots, zucchini, and cabbage. Every dieter needs a little solace, I believed, and Bea did seem to enjoy the veggies, especially the lettuce. She received it with a welcoming chomp of teeth, then carried it to the living room and crunched happily. The leaves had to be crisp, though. If I tried to sneak in a flaccid one by wrapping crisp ones around it, she'd spit it out and leave it on the floor.

Unfortunately, the vegetables were the only part of the new program that appealed to Bea. The rest decidedly displeased her. It became almost a personal crusade for her to resist the rules about her new diet. She repeatedly made it clear that there was no way she was going to give up being a black hole for food. John and I would have to concede to the stand she was taking, she informed us, and with fervor she began voicing her opposition to what we were (or were not) feeding her.

Bea began foraging lawlessly through the house. She raided Tigger's bowl with such abandon that we had to move the bowl from the bathroom counter's edge to the back of the sink, where Bea couldn't reach. She stole the food that I would set out for the homeless dogs and cats who were often dumped on our rural road. Bea, usually so polite to guests, showed no qualms about shoving these visitors aside and gulping down their dinners. To foil her, I had to feed them in a separate, closed-off room.

If there was no food to be found in the bowls of her fellow household occupants, Bea would turn to other means of satisfaction. She snatched papers from the wastebasket and sneaked them under the bed for a repast. She ate the leaves of potted plants and the fuzz off Ludwig's tennis balls. Over several weeks, a little at a time, she chewed her wicker bed and reduced the flat weave of its side to a row of spears the size of pencils.

Bea's oral fixation became more intense when John and I planted a garden. For two weekends, we double-dug a plot of earth behind the house, mixed in steer manure and leaf mold, and then planted lettuce, cucumbers, chard, eggplants, tomatoes, zucchini, and green beans. With excitement and anticipation we watched our garden grow until, finally, one night we carried a basket to our plot to gather our dinner salad. But instead of the flourishing lettuce heads we expected to harvest, we found only green nubs.

Bea, as you probably guessed, was the culprit. Standing in the chimney's shadow on the patio, she even looked guilty. Her back seemed extra-swayed, and she was showing inordinate interest in the hose nozzle. The temptation of lettuce had simply been too much for her, she seemed to be admitting, and her hunger had driven her to new criminal activity. She actually looked like she wanted to apologize.

But her remorse was short-lived, and she soon struck again. Before we could build a Bea-proof fence around our garden, she went after the chard. The beans were next; she grazed among the poles and nibbled the plants clear to the ground. Then she ate the cucumber vine, which didn't even have a chance to bloom. In the end, we gave up and turned the garden over to her. All she left for us were zucchini and tomatoes. She apparently preferred not to poke her nose among the stiff leaves, and she must have disliked the spurts of juice that erupted when she took bites.

Until this point, we'd either found ways of working around Bea's obsession, or accepted her plundering as a harmless irritation. But as months of dieting went by and she began to lose a little weight, she intensified her raids; and her behavior led to escalating crises.

One morning, as we were loading John's truck for a camping trip, I left our packed ice chest at the front door. On silent paws, Bea sneaked up, nosed open the lid, and ate two sticks of butter. All she left were two oily, shredded wrappers. On our drive up the winding California coast, she staggered to the front of the truck bed, stuck her head through the open window to the cab, and heaved butter down John's back.

Bea also managed to open the kitchen cabinet, where her kibble was stored in a plastic container. She worked off the cover and dove in for an orgy—and got so sick that late at night we had to take her to the emergency clinic. The vet diagnosed pancreatitis, and Bea spent several extremely worrisome days in the hospital. Afraid that she might repeat the kibble overdose when she got home, we installed special latches on the cabinet doors.

Even with these precautions, we couldn't keep up with Bea's relentless quest for food. One night we came home from a party and found that she had tossed aside a rug and snacked on two square feet of padding. Again, we rushed her to the clinic in the middle of the night. The threads stitched into the rubber could have easily come loose and gathered Bea's intestines like fabric at a skirt waistband, the vet told us—and Bea could easily die. John and I were so frightened that we couldn't even be mad at her. We left her at the clinic for the night, and the next morning we picked her up and took her to Andrew. He anesthetized her and pulled all the pieces of rubber pad from her stomach with an endoscope.

Relief was just one of our emotions. We also felt enormous gratitude that she'd been saved—and regret about our shortcomings, because the more John and I reflected on how close we'd come to losing Bea, the more we saw that she wasn't the only one at fault. By nearly dying, Bea had finally gotten through to us that we'd been as compulsive about her dieting as she'd been about her pillaging. We'd been too strict in forcing her to lose weight—and, if we'd learned nothing else during our years with her, we'd learned that nobody forces a beagle to do anything.

What became clear to us was that a chubby beagle was infinitely better than no beagle at all. To keep her safe, we were going to have to lower our expectations, defuse the conflict, and put an end to our battle of wills. In other words, to get along under one roof, we were all—Bea included—going to have to compromise.

Our solution was to find the middle ground between her obstinacy and our rigidity. So, our house turned into a spawning ground for the Golden Mean. We went back to giving Bea biscuits, but rather than a whole box of medium-sized ones each week, we carefully doled out only small ones, broken in half, interspersed with carrots and lettuce. We spooned a little more food into her bowl at each meal; and when we ate supper, we left her in the bed-room with Ludwig, so she wouldn't be tempted to melt our resolve with dramas of starvation.

Bea, too, seemed to understand the need for moderation, and she met us halfway. Maybe the endoscope experience had frightened her as much as it had us, and taught her that she had to end her days of theft and brashness. Or maybe she simply realized that she was no longer able to break into the kibble, so she graciously gave up the fight. Whatever her reasons, she never ate another rug pad, and she seemed to become less orally frenetic. Pounds did not melt off her, but she gained no weight. And harmony reigned in our house again.

# 9

# Our Distinguished Elder

In the next several years, Bea began to show her age, and she became a frail dowager who commanded deference. She trundled stiffly around the house on arthritic legs, and her muzzle grizzled, then turned completely white. When she woke, it would stay misshapen for a while from having been pressed flat on one side against her pillow. Her nose lost some of its pigment. Instead of looking like a licorice gumdrop, as it had all her life, it now reminded John and me of a pebble.

Soon all of Bea's coat had turned white. She would enter rooms like a phantom beagle. When John, whose own hair had turned prematurely gray, would take Bea for walks, people often stopped and noted how perfectly they matched, as if they'd shared a sudden fright and gone instantly gray together from the shock.

Far more frequently, however, people said that Bea looked like an angel. I would hear this comment especially often in the clinic waiting room of Jan

*John and Bea*

Lowry, the lovely, kind veterinarian we found nearby when Bea became too fragile for the long drive to Andrew. Drawn to Bea, strangers would get up from their seats and cross the room to pet her, then discuss her appearance. Not only did she appear to be wearing a white robe—after a bath, her fur seemed to shine more than white, like light—but, even with strangers, she had an exceptionally benign and loving presence.

I became especially aware of Bea's seraph tendencies one Indian-summer night when she must have been about fourteen. John and I had just gone to bed; he'd quickly fallen asleep, but I'd lain there for at least an hour stewing about an article I was writing. At that time I was cranking out work on topics that mattered little to me, just so I could write for what I believed were increasingly prestigious newspapers and magazines. My life was all about competing and climbing and finding ways to please my editors—and not myself.

The night was hot, the still, windless kind of night that you endure while hoping the early morning will usher in a little fog. I lay there watching the camellia bushes, silver in the moonlight, and listening to tree frogs and Bea's soft snores. As adept at lolling at night as during the day, she was sleeping in her poured-on-the-pillow position in her usual spot at the foot of the bed. Tigger was curled up in a ball in the crook behind my knees, and Ludwig was sprawled out, like a sultan, on the oriental rug. As usual, our bedroom seemed like a small, peaceful kennel.

Suddenly I heard a loud crackling, almost like a rifle being fired in the yard. Then another. And another. The sounds *were* shots. And they kept coming.

I bolted up in bed so frightened that my heart felt like it would pound out of my chest. All my life I'd heard about my relatives fleeing Russia during the 1917 revolution. Stories of cannon blasts and firing squads—and my grandmother and aunt escaping by ship as mines exploded all around them—had conditioned me, when surprised by shots, to expect a military end of me. The first thought that came to my panicked mind was that troops of Bolsheviks had gathered for an execution in my driveway.

Though rationality quickly returned, security did not.

I shook John's shoulder to wake him, but his eyes were already wide open. "We have to call nine-one-one!" I said. I jumped out of bed and stepped over Bea to grab the phone. The shots hadn't startled her into a seizure, I was glad to see, but she'd gotten to her feet and was standing by her pillow, looking confused and unsettled by all the commotion.

I tried to control my quivery voice as I described the gunshots to a dispatcher. "The sheriff is on his way. Don't worry," she said. Minutes later, a fleet of police cars and fire trucks arrived at our mailbox, about a football field's distance from our house. The police quickly shut down the road. From our bedroom window, John and I could make out only shadowy figures before revolving red lights. Then flashlight beams started moving slowly through the woods toward us.

In staccato whispers, John and I tried to figure out how best to keep the killers from coming to our house. Turn on the outdoor lights? Or stay hidden in the darkness with hopes no one would know that we were there? Before we could decide, someone knocked on the front door—and greatly magnified our fears. It was the sheriff, come to reassure us that no murderers were in our woods. But, he informed us, a man *had* just been shot on our dark, deserted road.

The sheriff kept telling us not to be alarmed, but that wasn't enough to bolster my anemic courage or warm my icy hands. The lights set up to illuminate the crime scene and the voices of policemen so close by didn't stop my fearful shivers either. From Bea, I'd learned all too well how a sudden fright could be hard to shake, and mine was sticking to me like the most tenacious lint.

Bea seemed immediately to perceive my distress—and to want to help. So resilient for a geriatric dog, she dismissed her confusion, got up from her pillow, and jumped into my lap. Rather than draping herself over my knees, as she usually did, she rooted against me, nestled against my chest, and rested her head on my neck, as if she were trying to guard as much of me as she could reach with her small body. Though she had no arms with which to hug and comfort me, she was doing the best she could with what she had.

Breathing in and out in sync with her, I felt immediately at peace. Our bond, I realized, had come full circle. Bea was showing me the most beautiful kindness: Instead of me taking care of her, as I'd been doing for years, I saw without a doubt that she was taking care of me. I was also certain that my well-being had come to matter as much to her as hers had always mattered to me. I remembered the message Abraham Lincoln had engraved in Mary Todd's wedding ring: "Love is eternal"—and now understood that the sentiment could apply to the deep affection not just between two people, but also between a person and an animal.

◘

OVER THE NEXT FEW YEARS, Bea became a centenarian in dog time. Age seemed to turn her, as it does many elderly dogs, into an old soul. She seemed almost to radiate the wisdom that can come from the cumulative experience of a long life. Besides being our resident angel, she became our venerable old sage.

Having her around was like sharing the house with an amiable grandmother knitting in her rocker and knowingly observing the folly around her. And the folly Bea observed was my often frantic, driven life of constant work. In contrast, Bea was serene and self-contained. She seemed to represent a developmental phase that I was still too young or blind to see. Though I recognized and valued her maturity, the example she set did not change my own pace and lifestyle.

One September, John and I decided we needed a vacation. Bea was now too frail to be left in the kennel, so we arranged for our friend Suzanne, a veterinary technician, to stay with

*Our resident sage*

her in our house. We rented a rustic cabin on San Juan Island in Washington, and for the first day we did little but sit and watch the seagulls and the sun, flashing diamonds on the water.

The next morning, I sat down on a bench in the bathroom to put on my socks. Whoever had last mopped the floor had pushed the props almost out from under the bench, so it was not securely supported, and under my weight, the bench—and I—crashed to the floor. As I lay there blinking at the stars whirling before my eyes, I felt as if my spine had been rammed through my skull and a Mack truck had run over my body. X rays and an MRI revealed that I had badly injured four disks, and for the next eight months, I lay on my office sofa in debilitating pain.

Day after day, I stared out the window, firmly convinced that I would never be able to work—or do much of anything—again. Besides the pain, the only constant in my life for all those months was Bea. She would lie on the floor next to the sofa, close enough for me to rest my hand on her for consolation. Or she would jump up and cuddle with me, just as she had after the man had been murdered on our road. Except for quick trips outside or to the kitchen for meals, Bea stayed with me every minute of the day, every single day. I knew she was there—constantly, unswervingly, loyally.

And generously. I didn't just lie there suffering in silence with an unresponsive lump of a dog. Bea was constantly engaged, actively reassuring me by her presence that, no matter how grouchy or depressed I got, she wouldn't leave me. Often I would talk, and she would listen, or we would have long, meandering conversations, in which I'd tell her about my misery, and, with nuzzles to my hand or bongo tail thumps against the sofa, she'd seem to try to buck me up.

From her years in a cage, I believed, she understood better than anyone how hopeless and trapped I felt. Whenever I looked at her, though, what I drew from her life's example was how possible it is to recover from a setback and to forgive. If she could let go of her harsh early life, I could stop hating the person who'd knocked the props from under the bench. Anger served no useful purpose, is what Bea's wagging tail said to me.

She also managed to do what my precocious ten-year-old friend Wolfie once suggested could be the reason for dogs' evolution: "to guide humans to their higher purpose." As I stroked Bea's white, velvet ears and talked with her day after day, my mind circled the question that often crops up when we are forced to admit to ourselves, perhaps for the first time, that our energy, strength, and years on earth are finite. And that question is: What is the meaning of life?

Wise little Buddha that Bea was, she snuggled up and reminded me by her own behavior that meaning lies in loving all we can and giving what we have to help others.

Perhaps that was a basic, universal, one-size-fits-all definition of "meaning," including for beagles, but how did it apply specifically to me? Bea, lying there so faithfully, nudged me to an answer. I realized that one of the main things I loved was her—and, in a more general sense, all animals. And one of the best ways I could spend my remaining years on the planet would be to put my love of animals into my writing and try in some small way to improve their lives.

As a freelance writer, I admitted, I had been frittering away my time and chasing all the wrong things for all the wrong reasons. Bea helped me see that I'd never be successful in any ultimate sense without being true to myself, just as she was true to her loving beagle nature. As Mother Teresa once said, "We're not called to be successful. We're called to be faithful,"—and that, I decided, includes being faithful to our abilities and deepest concerns. If I ever got strong enough to work again, I promised Bea, I would align my heart with my career.

◘

HAPPILY, when April arrived, strength and energy began to course through me again. Though my back still hurt, the pain no longer mowed me down, and I was able to work for a few hours every morning. Bea now became my life coach. The new job she took for herself was to stand by and encourage me as I worked toward my goals.

I asked my editors if they'd be interested in articles on animals, and two of them, surprisingly, answered, "Yes." As I quickly learned, being true to myself immediately led me to a joyful sense of purpose and freedom. Doors I'd never even imagined existed suddenly opened, and I got assignments that led to exciting adventures—and to the opportunity of making important points about animal welfare.

I decided to write about bats because I wanted to convey that they are not creepy, malevolent creatures, and that they should not be abused or unnecessarily killed. Bats actually perform crucial services for us—pollinating flowers, scattering seeds, propagating forests, and dining on pests that ravage agricultural crops, such as sugar cane and cotton. (Some kinds of bats eat up to 2,000 mosquito-sized insects in just one night.) At a cave near San Antonio, Texas, I watched tens of thousands of bats emerge into the night, like huge, billowing clouds of smoke. Collectively, their tiny wings roared like Niagara Falls.

For a week in Montana, I followed a magnificent grizzly bear named Lacy with a team of biologists who were teaching her not to scavenge in garbage cans. We set up ambushes for her in orchards, along a highway, and on a back porch where she'd been raiding birdseed and kibble. Rubber bullets and cracker shells sent Lacy running from these forbidden places and conveyed to her that she must stay away from people. This may have ultimately saved her from having to be destroyed: In my article, I made sure to point out how we jeopardize bears when we leave out enticing food.

I also went to Tennessee to visit Osceola, an eagle, whose wing had been shot for target practice by a hunter. The raptor's keeper had made a little harness for him and taken him hang-gliding, so he could experience again the joy of flying and of wind ruffling his feathers. Osceola stared at me with a piercing, regal gaze and practically commanded me to let the world know the tragedy that can result from taking potshots for fun at any bird, much less our nation's symbol. My work on that article, I told myself, would be more than worthwhile if my words made just one sportsman stop and reconsider before taking needless aim at a bird.

On all these and other trips for my new work, Bea's spirit was always with me. When I got home, she was always waiting for me. As I wrote my articles, she would lie at my feet, and her presence encouraged me to keep my values straight. She reminded me to stay on the path she had helped me find.

By being so loving, Bea also kept suggesting that I shouldn't forget about animal kindness, so I got out files of stories I'd collected a few years before and started writing my first book, *The Compassion of Animals*. I began to do interviews and was astonished by what the people I spoke with had to say: More than half of them felt that their animal had been an angel in their lives. This comment came from burly firemen and state troopers, not just the gentle souls one would expect to make the observation. Often people would weep with gratitude or wonder at the kindness that an animal had shown them. To all of them, believing or not believing in angels seemed beside the point. They mainly wanted to convey to me how their dog, cat, horse, or parrot had watched over them, guarded them, protected them, comforted them, guided them, encouraged them, or intervened for them.

That's just what Bea had been doing for me in her wise and kindly senior years. So eager to help, she'd proven herself to be a highly celestial sort of dog. As she got even older—and whiter—she would lie on her pillow in my office or on the floor at the foot of the bed, and John and I would feel her consoling, loving spirit. In her quiet, unobtrusive way, Bea gave new meaning to the notion of an angel in the house.

# 10

# Death and Rebirth

By THE TIME BEA HAD lived with us for fifteen years, she was reaching a phenomenal old age for a beagle. If you added the five years that Andrew had estimated her age on her first visit to his clinic, Bea would have been about twenty years old—or, in human terms, around one hundred and forty, right up there with Abraham and Sarah in Genesis.

Life was getting harder and harder for Bea. She would struggle to her feet and hobble to the kitchen for her supper, then heave herself down on her pillow again with a heavy, weary sigh. She ate less than she once did, never barked, and withdrew into an ever-shrinking world, while largely ignoring Anna and Linguine, the German shepherd and tabby cat who had joined our family after Ludwig and Tigger had peacefully died.

Then, in addition to becoming even more physically frail, Bea began to develop serious medical problems. All her systems seemed to break down at once. Her new vet, Jan Lowry, nursed her through kidney failure, an ulcerated colon, thyroid trouble, deafness, and near-blindness. On some days Bea took almost a dozen pills for her various ailments.

One afternoon, while Bea was having blood drawn for a lab test, Carol, the clinic's business manager, took me aside in the reception area. "We're keeping Bea alive with baling wire and Scotch tape," she said, and put her arm around my shoulder. I knew that she was trying to prepare me for the inevitable. John and I would have to brace ourselves to see Bea through her death with the love and kindness she deserved.

We were crushed by the grief that we anticipated, and so, to bolster our spirits, at night while Bea slept at the foot of our bed, we would whisper about all the good times we'd had with her. We would softly laugh about our Boogle Woogle's fat pads, her "grrrrmmmms," her once-used toothbrush, her butter theft, her raccoon blood-lust, her hotdog rewards for puddles, her tail's Metronome and Swish.

"How can we live without her?" I would ask John.

He never had an answer.

*Bea, a week before she died*

Living without Bea was unthinkable because she'd had such a profound effect on us—an effect that was still deepening. She hadn't simply recovered from the trauma of her origins; she'd gone on to become what we believed was the world's finest dog—teaching us, along the way, how goodness is to be found in the most desolate places; that the lowly or the unattractive deserve their beauty coaxed from them; that if given a chance, the world can right itself, turning bad to good. She'd helped us learn patience and the importance of never giving up. She'd bolstered our faith and enabled us to see that things we can't control can still turn out all right.

But mostly, Bea had taught us about love. Sometimes I thought of her as a fur-wrapped, special-delivery package, sent from the cosmos solely to wake John and me up to love's extraordinary power—which, we now knew, could come most magnificently even from a small dog. Bea had given us so much more than we ever gave her, and she had loved us with such intensity and fervor.

Sometimes our evening whispers included a discussion of whether it was "time." As long as Bea was not suffering and was still getting some pleasure out of life, we agreed, it was *not* time. We would list all the ways that Bea still found happiness: in her meals, her sprawls in the patch of sun below the skylight, the biscuits she crunched with her few remaining teeth, her pillow fluffed up in front of the fireplace. John and I constantly sought more things to add to the list because the longer it was, the longer it seemed that Bea would live.

Though we couldn't postpone our loss forever, we kept telling each other that Bea would let us know when she wanted to leave. And, finally, she did. One afternoon she started having seizures nearly every half-hour, and between them, she would restlessly pace the house. With sorrow and dismay, we followed her as she moved from room to room. "She looks like she's trying to find her way home," John said.

That was exactly what Bea was doing. It was time to help her get there.

I called Jan, who had promised to come and put Bea down in her own bed in order to save her a trip to the clinic when she was so weak and sick. While we waited, we tried to feed Bea ice cream and biscuits, but she wasn't interested. I took her for a final visit to her forest and told her again and again how much I loved her and what a gift she had been to me. Even though she probably couldn't hear my words, I believe that she heard me on some level. I could tell, though, that her mind was drifting away.

Jan finally got to our house. With great kindness, she placed Bea on her pillow and gave her an injection. As our tears plopped down on the denim around her, Bea seemed to sink into herself. Then, in the last moment before her heart stopped beating, she raised her head. Though she'd been completely silent for a year, she let out a final, amazing, joyful "arrooo!" Bea had met death, just as she'd met life, with a good bark.

What, if anything, had prompted it? Perhaps she'd been barking at celestial rabbits, John suggested. In Jan's opinion, it was completely to be expected that such a spunky little dog as Bea would leave the earth in such a manner. My hope was that at the very end she was greeting the next life with the confidence we'd worked so hard to coax out of her in this one. I wanted to think of Bea running and barking, with her ears flapping in the wind through heavenly forests and meadows.

◘

FOR DAYS AFTER Bea's death, our house felt as if it were wrapped tightly in a black veil. Everything seemed muffled, restrained, and dark. Though John and I were certain that Bea had moved on to a better place, free of the restraints of sickness and age, we missed her terribly.

Together, we put Bea's bowl and pillows in the garage.
We washed her last nose-prints from the French doors in
my office, and I brought what was left of her pills to Jan
to give to animals whose guardians couldn't afford to buy
medications. With white thread, I tied together a few of
Bea's whiskers and her tail tip's cowlick whorl, which I
had asked Jan to trim from Bea's body, and I put them
with her dog tag in a special memorial box.

John and I set about trying to get back to a normal
life, but sometimes sadness would reassert itself despite
our determined efforts. I would think I heard Bea snoring
her gargled-pebble snore. Or at night I would get up and
step over what I perceived to be her body, lying in the
spot where she'd always slept at the foot of the bed. In the
kitchen, I would reach down to pour kibble into a bowl
that was no longer there. Each time, with a jolt of recog-
nition, I remembered that Bea was gone.

Then, a week later, almost to the hour of Bea's death,
something extraordinary happened. I was working in my
office, feeling alone and desolate, when I heard shrieks
and cries outside my window. Certain that a speeding car
had hit an animal, as often happened on my rural road, I
rushed outside. I found nothing. Then I heard the cries
again, coming from farther away. Perhaps the injured animal had dragged itself to a field across the road, I thought.
Walking toward the field, I rounded a bend, and what I
saw took my breath away.

A small beagle was running down the trail toward me. Her paws flew over the dirt, and she held her tail firmly in an upright smile. I stooped down to meet her; and she threw herself into my arms, as if she'd been searching the world for me. She was quite young, painfully thin, and absolutely filthy, her paws red and miserably swollen, and her fur covered with ticks.

Either this dog was lost and had been roaming the streets for a while, or someone had badly neglected her — and perhaps that very day had dumped her on my road. I would never know her origins. But one thing I was sure of: From this point on, nothing on earth could have taken her from me. Even if her guardian had suddenly appeared, aimed a gun at me, and demanded her back, I would not have relinquished her. Hugging her as if I, too, had been searching the world for her, I asked, "Did Bea send you?"

*Phoebe Miracle*

Of course, Bea did. Or so I want to believe. I like to think that animals and people, even after death, can

continue to love us
and look out for us.
Anything is possible.

I crossed the road
and brought the dog
home. I set her on the
kitchen floor and gave
her a whole can of dog
food, which she de-
voured as if she hadn't
been fed for weeks.
Then, despite her thrashing and wriggling, I bathed her
to remove her layer of dirt so she could run freely
through the house. Finally, I wrapped her in a towel
and sat down in my white wicker rocking chair with
her. In a few minutes, she fell asleep, her chin resting on
my arm.

When I telephoned John at work to tell him that I had
found another beagle, he didn't hesitate for an eyeblink before agreeing that we should keep her. I took her to Jan
to have the ticks removed; and when our vet opened the
exam room's door and found me sitting there with a new
beagle on my lap, her face froze with surprise. The vet
techs and the office staff, who had been so kind to Bea in
her last years, all crowded together, telling joyful stories of
animals who had been lost or abandoned, then found their
way to good homes.

Petting our new beagle, Jan kept saying, "You lucky, lucky dog." No, I told her. "I'm the lucky one."

When I picked our beagle up after her treatment at the clinic, she was wearing a red plaid bandanna and practically bristling with hope and cheer. As I drove her home, I kept thinking of the endless cycles of life—of birth, death, and rebirth. There was something eternal going on with Bea and this new beagle, I believed. Her name, John and I decided, would be Phoebe Miracle—Phoebe because the "be" echoed our Bea. And Miracle because that was exactly what her arrival in our life had been—just like Bea.

*Postscript*

# A Final Lesson
# from Bea

I BELIEVE THAT MOST things happen for a reason, and one reason Bea may have come into my life was to encourage me to think about lab animals. Needless to say, they'd always been a topic that I wanted to avoid. But as Eleanor Roosevelt once said, "You must do the thing you think you cannot do." For me, that was to learn about the animals—and especially beagles—and come to an informed, rather than simply emotional, opinion about them. I felt I had to do it for Bea.

The number of animals used every year for research, education, and testing was staggering to me, even though I was told that the number has been coming down. Worldwide, the estimate is 60 to 70 million animals annually. In the United States it's 20 million, but the total is thought to be much higher because numbers for frogs and fish are unavailable, and federal reporting requirements don't include birds — or mice and rats, by far the two most common experimental animals. In 1999, more than 75,000 dogs, many of whom were beagles, were used in U.S. labs.

Most of the animals come from commercial suppliers who breed them specifically for laboratories, and some animals are captured in the wild and sold for research. Approximately 50 percent of laboratory dogs and cats are taken from shelters in a process called "pound seizure" or bought from brokers, who obtain them from newspaper ads or at trade auctions, much like outdoor flea markets. In these ways, a beagle who was formerly part of a human family can end up in experiments.

Physically, beagles are considered especially desirable for labs. The dogs' skeletons and bone marrow resemble those of humans, their genetic diversity is greater than that of other breeds, and they tend to be long-lived. Also, beagles' short hair is easily shaved for the tending and observing of surgical sites. For these reasons, medical students practice operations on them, and researchers commonly use them for cardiological, cardiovascular, and joint-replacement studies — and for transplant experiments.

Emotionally, beagles' main asset for labs is their friendly, gentle nature, which makes them easy to handle.

Yet they're also stoic and stubborn; they don't give up.
That may be partly why beagles were once used for extended studies on the effects of nuclear fallout by researchers, who called themselves the "Beagle Club." The
beagles were either fed a daily diet of strontium 90, in-
jected with radium, forced to inhale radioactive material,
irradiated with cobalt, or irradiated while pregnant so the
babies would be affected in the womb. These stalwart beagles did not buckle in the labs for years.

Because of beagles' physical and psychological traits,
they're especially popular with private companies that test
the efficacy and safety of various substances. Researchers
force the beagles to swallow, inject them with, or put into
their eyes pharmaceuticals, cosmetics, household products, chemicals, and pesticides — and then the researchers
see what happens, including whether the dogs die. In
one study, scientists gave male beagles Viagra, the
anti-impotency drug (which at the time was already
government-approved and being taken by humans). Then
the researchers removed the foreskins of the beagles'
penises, implanted electrodes, and administered electric
shocks to the nerves that cause an erection. After the firm-
ness of the dogs' penises was measured, the beagles were
put to death.

In the past, neither beagles nor any other lab animals
had legal protection. But in 1966, Pepper, a Dalmatian,
was rounded up in Missouri and sold for research, then

died before her human family could find her. After shocking photos of Pepper and other dogs appeared in *Life* magazine, angry readers wrote more letters to the magazine than for any article in its history—and more letters to Congress than for civil rights or the Vietnam War. The result of the outcry was the Animal Welfare Act, which authorized the Secretary of Agriculture to regulate the transport, sale, and handling of dogs, cats, nonhuman primates, guinea pigs, hamsters, and rabbits intended for research and other purposes.

But the Act did not go far enough. In 1985, at the Institute for Behavioral Research in Silver Springs, Maryland, macaques (small monkeys) were found chewing on their own limbs after nerves to the limbs had been severed in an experiment; and at the University of Pennsylvania Medical Center, videos were taken of lab employees teasing baboons whose heads had been crushed in trauma tests. When these incidents were publicized, another avalanche of angry letters persuaded Congress to pass new laws clarifying "humane care" for animals and regulating their sanitation, housing, and ventilation. The laws also specify that pain and distress should be minimized and that alternatives to animals should be considered in experiments. Most important, the amendment establishes that an Institutional Animal Care and Use Committee (IACUC) in every lab must oversee animal welfare and approve or disapprove research proposals according to federal regulations.

These laws lay the groundwork, but, unfortunately, they are not uniformly followed. Though some IACUCs provide even better animal care than is legally required, others provide far worse; and there are too few federal inspectors to check all the regulated labs. The committees also vary in what they do or don't allow to be done to animals. In one study, Scott Plous of Wesleyan University and Harold Herzog of Western Carolina University compared the judgments made by fifty randomly selected IACUCs on 150 recent research proposals to determine if the judgments were consistent. The results showed that they were not. In fact, decisions about whether or not to approve a procedure were statistically unrelated—as reliable as a coin toss—even if the proposed experiments meant pain or death for the animals. There were no universal standards.

As Martin Stevens, vice president of animal research issues at the Humane Society of the United States, told me, "We have laws and regulations in place that address the key issues of animals' pain and distress, and minimize suffering in principle. How well the laws and regulations work depends on how seriously they are taken." Sadly, that's sometimes not seriously enough, and animals needlessly suffer.

For Bea

◘

ALL MY LIFE, my heart had told me that research which inflicted hardship on animals was unethical and cruel. Then my mind would step in, wag an accusatory finger at me, and argue that maybe I could feel that way about using animals to test mascara or detergent, but I couldn't deny the importance of animals for medical progress. To save human lives, the animals' dismal existence was just something my intellect said I had to live with—and try to ignore. Animals simply had to be sacrificed, my heart be damned, and that was that.

Certainly, I myself have had plenty to thank lab animals for. Developed and tested on animals, vaccines have kept me from getting the flu in winter, and antibiotics have rescued me time and again from infections. I've traveled, carefree, throughout the world after immunizations against typhoid, hepatitis, cholera, and other diseases—immunizations that exist because of animals. When I injured my back, the pills I took for pain, also developed and tested on animals, were nothing less than miracles. Such medications also extended Bea's life, and gave me the incredible bonus of extra time with her. I would have been a hypocrite to deny the benefits I'd received from animal experiments, and I believed I was in no position to argue against them.

But the more I learned, the more I realized that even

in medicine or drug- and product-safety testing, animals
are not always the unqualified, essential, undeniable boon
I had believed they were. Research with them can be a
messy business, fraught with drawbacks, complications,
dead ends, false conclusions, and even danger to us — to
say nothing of ethical problems. Though some experts see
sun shining over laboratories, other experts point out
shadows looming.

Animals may have helped with medical advancement,
but they have also hindered it. For one thing, they've de-
layed it. In 1929, for example, Alexander Fleming discovered that penicillin killed bacteria in a Petri dish. When he
gave the compound to bacteria-infested rabbits, it did
nothing; so for a decade he stored the drug away. Only
when he gave it, as a last resort, to a dying man, who
hadn't responded to other treatments — and the man survived — did Fleming realize that the drug could heal humans. Experiments on rabbits long postponed that miracle
for us.

Lab animals have also led medical researchers down
blind alleys. In 1912, pathologists found the poliovirus in
human intestines, which suggested that it entered humans
through the digestive tract. But years later, when lab monkeys were infected with the virus through their noses, researchers concluded that humans got polio in the same
way — and started a long and fruitless direction of studies.
Finally, in 1941, Albert Sabin found through autopsies of

human polio victims that the virus was not in nasal mucus, but in the intestinal tract. Human, not monkey, research led to the accurate conclusion that ultimately made possible a vaccine against the disease.

Animal experiments may have alleviated misery and saved lives, but misunderstandings from those experiments have also had extremely destructive consequences. After heart-lung transplants were developed on dogs, for example, the first three human patients who underwent the surgery died within weeks; and of twenty-eight patients who had the transplants between 1981 and 1985, eight died within twenty-four hours of the operation, and ten developed obliterative bronchiolitis, a lung complication. Of those ten, four died and three needed a respirator to breathe for the rest of their lives. The dogs used in the research had never gotten obliterative bronchiolitis, and the work on them did not accurately predict what would happen to humans.

Misleading results from animal product-safety and drug tests have also had severe effects on us. Because smoking-related cancer was difficult to reproduce in animals, cigarettes were long believed to be benign for us. And because asbestos didn't cause cancer in animals at all, no one realized for years that it was lethal to humans. Drugs that have no damaging side effects in animals have often presented humans with serious risks. Thalidomide caused no birth defects in animals as it did in us, for in-

stance. The cardiac drug milrinone increased the recovery
of rats with induced heart attacks, but caused a 30-percent
increase in deaths of humans who had chronic heart failure and took the drug. Approximately 100,000 people are
said to die each year from drugs that proved safe in animal tests.

These examples are just the tiniest pinch in huge
fistfuls of arguments about the worth and legitimacy of
animals even in medical and safety experiments. As I read
more and talked with experts, I could see clearly that the
subject is extremely polarizing and complex—a massive,
ever-changing slippery slope that I could try to climb for
years, yet never know enough to make a sweeping and
conclusive judgment about it. Nevertheless, I did decide
that even potentially lifesaving animal experiments, for all
their plusses, are riddled with enough minuses to warrant
great caution and serious questions. I also finally decided
that whether animals should be used in labs at all is a question that's bigger than I am, one I should leave up to God.

At the same time, though, I came to two emphatic
beliefs:

One is that not nearly so many animals need to find
their way to labs as do today, and everything possible
should be done to lower the numbers.

Jerry Vlasak, a former researcher and now a surgeon
in Santa Monica, California, told me that no animal actually was needed even in medical labs today because animal

experiments are outdated. "Animals have no relevance to pertinent medical research in the twenty-first century," he said. "It's like driving a Model T. We don't need to do that anymore." Though other researchers would disagree with him, no one can deny the existence of all the exciting alternatives that can replace lab animals entirely, or at least greatly diminish their numbers in specific tests and procedures.

Research can be done *in vitro* (in test tubes and Petri dishes) on human blood, tissue, organs, and cells—ideal ways to test the safety of viral vaccines, and to study the toxicity or efficacy of chemicals. Several substitutes have been developed for the Draize test, which requires putting a test substance into the eyes of rabbits, for instance. One is the agarose diffusion test: In a flask, the substance is placed over a layer of human cells, along with a thin cushion of a derivative of agar, taken from a sea plant, to keep the cells from being crushed. If the test material is an irritant, dead cells will appear around it. (Because of alternatives to the Draize test, determining eye irritation with animals is said to have fallen an estimated 87 percent in the United States cosmetics industry.)

Animals can be spared with breakthroughs in biotechnology, such as Robert Wood Johnson Medical School scientists' cloning human cells and bioengineering tissue to create living human skin. It can now be used instead of the practices of burning live animals for research models, and

of shaving their backs, applying test substances, and seeing how deeply the chemicals will corrode the animals'
skin.

Rather than giving animals diseases, then studying
ways to cure them, researchers can opt for clinical studies,
monitoring human patients who already have the illnesses,
and observing responses to treatments. Scientists can also
carry out epidemiological studies, comparing large popu-
lations of people to determine why they get or don't get a
specific illness. Breakthrough discoveries about human
health have come through these alternatives: how certain
chemical exposures can cause birth defects, how heart disease can be reversed by eating a low-fat diet and stopping
smoking, and how AIDS is transmitted and can be prevented—to name only a few.

New technologies also offer alternatives to lab animals in medical research. Computer modeling can simulate
living systems, chemical reactions, and complex disease
processes. (One computer program developed by the National Cancer Institute models relationships between the
human body's immune system and cancer—and has prevented millions of animals from having cancer induced in
them for experiments.) Modern noninvasive imaging de-
vices, such as ultrasound, nuclear magnetic resonance, and
CAT scanners, allow scientists to do research painlessly on
humans, rather than on animals, and to investigate animals' bodies without cutting into them while they're alive

or killing them to dissect them for data. Researchers at McLean Hospital in Belmont, Massachusetts, chose magnetic resonance angiography to determine, from the brains of twenty-four men who'd taken a low dose of cocaine, that even those doses constrict brain blood vessels and cause brain-cell loss. The technology saved twenty-four animals from being given cocaine and then killed for brain dissection.

Sometimes even simple technologies can serve as alternatives to animal use, especially in education. As an alternative to dissecting frogs and other animals, medical and science students can study anatomy and physiology with 3-D models—or more sophisticated interactive videos and computer simulations. Instead of forcing a tube repeatedly down a live dog's throat, firefighters can learn trauma-training techniques on manikins and human anatomical simulators. Rather than using live rats, medical students can practice microsurgery operation techniques on life-sized rat models with realistic latex organs and blood vessels. Since 1876, in England, surgeons have trained not on animals but on human cadavers, and then assisted experienced surgeons in operations.

These examples are only a small percentage of the available alternatives, and with more funding and support, still more could be developed. Now the challenge is to persuade all researchers to use them. As Martin Stevens told me, "We need to hold researchers' feet to the fire." And we must convince legislators to pass regulations requiring that any alternative developed for a given test or procedure be not just considered, as the law demands now, but actually used.

We also need to make absolutely certain that lab animals do not suffer. My second emphatic belief is that every possible step should be taken to end—or at the very least greatly lessen—the animals' pain and distress, including their anxiety, fear, and depression. To me, that's more than simply a matter of compassion; it's a moral obligation.

Unfortunately, animals do suffer pain, and sometimes it must be overwhelming. At the Physicians Committee for Responsible Medicine, researcher Robert Eckstein studied the fate of dogs used in fifty-two experiments chosen at random from scientific literature. He found that ten days was the median length for an experiment, though 32 percent of them went on for a month and one experiment lasted for five and a half years. Sixty-three percent of those experiments caused the dogs significant pain, and 13 percent, which were performed without anesthetics, caused severe pain.

The truth is that lab animals don't always get necessary anesthetics or analgesics, especially when recovering from surgeries. Nor are the animals always given sedatives or anti-anxiety medications when experiments are emotionally upsetting. And animals are frequently studied until they die (with death as the end-point of the experi-

For Bea

ment), and no one is around to monitor their breathing and pulse rate and make sure that they are not deteriorating quickly or suffering more than was anticipated, or to observe early indicators of approaching death and put them down once death becomes inevitable. Experimental procedures need to be made more humane whenever possible, and animals always need to be provided with medications that alleviate their suffering. Ongoing concern and attentiveness to their pain and distress seems to me the least we can do to repay them for what they do for us.

I have also come to believe that animals' psychological well-being deserves far more consideration than it is now given. From knowing Bea, I can say with authority that beagles need freedom from small cages and plenty of room to romp around with their friends. Beagles need to be played with, cuddled, reassured, given toys, fed comforting food—as do all experimental animals. If I had my way, once they had served their purpose, they'd be adopted, if possible, by someone who would continue to appreciate and care for them—and show them gratitude for having been veterans in a war they did not choose.

◘

AS I READ and interviewed experts about lab animals, I was often nearly overcome with grief. Even doing the research in honor of Bea was not enough to compensate for my worry and sadness. But I did take heart in learning that

I'm not alone in my concern about lab animals' welfare. Attitudes are changing, and an ever-increasing number of people want the animals not to suffer or to be used in unrestricted or inessential experiments. In 1985, 63 percent of Americans polled said they believed that scientists should be allowed to cause pain and injury to animals if it produced information of benefit to human health. In 1996, only 50 percent believed it. In a recent Humane Society of the United States study, a majority of Americans approved using animals only for tests that are crucial, wanted lab animals' lives improved with stronger federal regulations, and believed that alternatives to lab animals should be developed and promoted. In a recent Zogby poll, 51 percent of Americans said they felt that primates, frequently used in labs, deserved the same rights as human children.

Those statistics give me hope. Even though I can't wave a magic wand and free all lab animals this very minute—or at least guarantee them comfort—I believe that the day will come when no animal will ever be forced into a lab again. While I wait and work for that day, even if it doesn't come in my own lifetime, I will try to remember to stay as stubbornly determined, and yet as optimistic, as Bea or Phoebe—or any beagle.

Phoebe is presently running around behind my house, sniffing the ground with unabashed confidence that somehow she is going to find the raccoon who sauntered through the yard last night and left a scented trail. Occasionally Phoebe raises her head, wags her tail, and howls an earnest and cheerful "arroooo" to greet passersby along the street. But then she gets back to work, clearly determined to figure out just where that raccoon might be hiding, so she can tree it. Nothing could distract her for long from her serious mission.

No matter what objective Phoebe has, she never relents or gets discouraged. She keeps the faith that victory is waiting, not so very far away. As she goes about her task, she also exudes a beagle's loving spirit; and she keeps her tail raised and proudly waves its white "flag" (as beaglers call the tail's tip), just as Bea did. When it comes to how any of us should work for a cause—or even live our lives—a beagle's tail in its sideways smile says it all.

*Appendix*

# What You Can Do

$W$HEN I TALK ABOUT
trying to improve the lives of lab animals, someone often asks
with hopelessness, "As just one person, what can I possibly do
for them?" The answer is "Plenty." Single voices can add up to
an influential roar, made all the louder if they're the voices of
people who live according to what Mahatma Gandhi once suggested: "You must be the change you wish to see in the world."
There are many ways to "be the change" for lab animals.

• Buy the products and stock of companies with animal-
friendly policies. Look for products whose labels contain such
phrases as "cruelty-free" and "no animal testing." If you have
questions about a company's practices, call its public-relations

director or its toll-free customer-information number. (For a list of companies that have adopted the "Corporate Standard of Compassion for Animals," given by the Coalition for Consumer Information on Cosmetics, see http://www.leapingbunny. org/shopping_guide.htm.)

• Keep lab animals in mind when making charitable donations. Support national organizations working for the animals' welfare—the Physicians Committee for Responsible Medicine, People for the Ethical Treatment of Animals, or the Humane Society of the United States, to name only a few. Or give to cruelty-free charities, such as Easter Seals, rather than to those, like the March of Dimes, that still fund experiments with animals rather than alternatives. (For a list of charities that do or do not support animal research, look at the Physicians Committee for Responsible Medicine's www.charitiesinfo. org.) Before donating to your alma mater or to any school of higher education, find out if their policies about animal research are compatible with your views. A good place to begin with your questions would be a letter to the dean of science or vice president for research.

• Join a national or local animal-advocacy group that works for lab animals. (To find a list of organizations, see www.animalsagenda.org.)

• If you're a student, refuse to dissect or experiment on an animal. If you're the parent of a child attending a high school where animals are used in labs, join the PTA to encourage the adoption of the many and readily available alternatives. Know that some states legally require teachers to let students use them without being penalized. (For information, including where you can obtain the alternatives, contact the National Anti-Vivisection Society's Dissection Hotline at 800-922-FROG.)

• If you want to get directly involved with lab animals, ask to tour the labs of companies and research facilities. (Taxpayer-funded facilities are legally required to let you inside.) If you don't like what you see, you can speak out, or even volunteer to become a member of the lab's Institutional Animal Care and Use Committee, which is required by law to have one representative from the community. By being on the committee, you can influence how the animals are treated.

• Stay informed about the issues. A good place to get information is from the websites of major organizations concerned with lab animal welfare, including:

Animal Legal Defense Fund: www.aldf.org
Association of Veterinarians for Animals Rights:
    www.avar.org
In Defense of Animals: www.idausa.org
Johns Hopkins University's Center for Alternatives
    to Animal Testing: altweb.jhsph.edu
Medical Research Modernization Committee:
    www.mrmcmed.org
National Anti-Vivisection Society: www.navs.org
Physicians Committee for Responsible Medicine:
    www.pcrm.org

# Appendix

People for the Ethical Treatment of Animals:

    www.peta-online.org

Humane Society of the United States:

    www.hsus.org

To get information on federally funded animal-research projects, you can contact the Freedom of Information Act Office at www.nih.gov/icd/od/foia/. And to learn specifics about all research proposals, funding, and facilities, look at Computer Retrieval Information on Scientific Projects (CRISP) at http://crisp.cit.nih.gov/.

• Let your voice be heard. Call or write letters to companies, research institutions, regulatory agencies, and the editor of your local paper. When federal or state legislative battles are being waged over pound seizure, the treatment of nonhuman primates, and other lab-animal issues, pressure the politicians. Encourage them to tighten laws about animal research.

# Suggested Reading

Arluke, Arnold, and C. R. Sanders. 1996. *Regarding Animals*. Philadelphia: Temple University Press.

Beck, Alan, and Aaron Katcher. 1996. *Between Pets and People: The Importance of Animal Companionship*. West Lafayette, Indiana: Purdue University Press.

Bestrup, Craig. 1998. *Disposable Animals: Ending the Tragedy of Throwaway Pets*. Leander, Texas: Camino Bay Books.

Blum, Deborah. 1994. *The Monkey Wars*. New York: Oxford University Press.

Colombo, Henry, A. D. Holcombe, Lew Madden, Owen Payne, and Morgan Wing, Jr. 1975. *The New Complete Beagle*. New York: Howell Book House Inc.

Davis, Hank, and Dianne Balfour, eds. 1992. *The Inevitable*

*Bond: Examining Scientist-Animal Interactions.* Cambridge, England: Cambridge University Press.

Dunbar, Ian, ed. 1999. *The Essential Beagle.* New York: Howell Book House.

Fox, Michael F. W. 1986. *Laboratory Animal Husbandry: Ethology, Welfare, and Experimental Variables.* Albany, New York: State University of New York Press.

Francione, Gary L. 2000. *Introduction to Animal Rights: Your Child or the Dog.* Philadelphia: Temple University Press.

Francione, Gary L., and Anna E. Charlton. 1992. *Vivisection and Dissection in the Classroom: A Guide to Conscientious Objection.* Jenkintown, Pennsylvania: American Anti-Vivisection Society.

Garner, Robert. 1993. *Animals, Politics, and Morality.* New York: St. Martin's Press.

Gray, Thelma. 1980. *The Beagle.* London: Popular Dogs.

Hepner, Lisa A. 1994. *Animals in Education: The Facts, Issues, and Implications.* Albuquerque: Richmond Publishers.

Hobson, J. C. Jeremy. 1987. *Beagling.* London: David & Charles.

Jasper, James. M., and Dorothy Nelkin. 1992. *The Animal Rights Crusade: The Growth of a Moral Protest.* New York: The Free Press.

LaFollette, Hugh, and Niall Shanks. 1996. *Brute Science: Dilemmas of Animal Experimentation.* London: Routledge.

Langley, Gill, ed. 1989. *Animal Experimentation: The Consensus Changes.* Houndmills, England: Macmillan.

Lewis, C.S. 1962. *The Problem of Pain.* New York: Collier Books.

Midgeley, Mary. 1998. *Animals and Why They Matter.* Athens, Georgia: University of Georgia Press.

Musladin, Judith, A. C. Musladin, and Ada T. Lueke. 1998. *The New Beagle.* New York: Howell Book House.

Nicholas, Anna Katherine, and Marcia Foy. *The Beagle.* Neptune City, New Jersey: T.F.H. Publications.

Orlans, F. Barbara. 1993. *In the Name of Science: Issues in Responsible Animal Experimentation.* New York: Oxford University Press.

Palika, Liz. 2000. *How to Train Your Beagle.* Neptune City, New Jersey: Kingdom.

Parent, Lucia E. 1995. *Beagles.* Hauppauge, New York: Barron's.

Paton, William. 1993. *Man and Mouse: Animals in Medical Research.* 2nd ed. Oxford, England: Oxford University Press.

Pisano, Beverly, and A. D. Holcombe. 1988. *Beagles.* Neptune City, New Jersey: T.F.H. Publications.

Regan, Tom, ed. 1986. *Animal Sacrifices: Religious Perspectives on the Use of Animals in Science.* Philadelphia: Temple University Press.

Reitman, Judith. 1992. *Stolen for Profit: How the Medical Establishment Is Funding a National Pet-Theft Conspiracy.* New York: Pharos Books.

Rohr, J. L. 1989. *Animal Rights: Opposing Viewpoints.* San Diego: Greenhaven Press.

Rollin, Bernard E. 1989. *The Unheeded Cry: Animal Consciousness, Animal Pain, and Science.* Oxford, England: Oxford University Press.

Rowan, Andrew N. 1984. *Of Mice, Models, and Men: A Critical Evaluation of Animal Research.* Albany, New York: State University of New York Press.

Rowan, Andrew N., Franklin M. Loew, and Joan C. Weer. 1995. *The Animal Research Controversy: Protest, Process, and Public Policy.* Boston: Tufts University.

Ryder, Richard D. 1975. *Victims of Science.* London: Davis-Poynter.

Shapiro, Kenneth J. 1998. *Animal Models of Human Psychology: Critique of Science, Ethics, and Policy.* Seattle: Hogrefe and Huber.

Sharpe, Robert. 1988. *The Cruel Deception: The Use of Animals in Medical Research.* Wellingborough, England: Thorsons Publishing Group.

Singer, Peter. 1990. *Animal Liberation: A New Ethics for Our Treatment of Animals.* 2nd ed. New York: Random House.

Singer, Peter. 1998. *Ethics Into Action.* New York: Rowman & Littlefield.

Smith, Jane A., and Kenneth M. Boyd, eds. 1991. *Lives in the Balance: The Ethics of Using Animals in Biomedical Research.* Oxford, England: Oxford University Press.

Vallila, Andrew. 1999. *Beagle.* Philadelphia: Chelsea House.

Vyvyan, John. 1988. *In Pity and in Anger: A Study of the Use of Animals in Science.* Marblehead, Massachusetts: Micah Publications.

Wilcox, Charlotte. 1998. *The Beagle*. Mankato, Minnesota: Capstone Press.

Wise, Steven M. 2000. *Drawing the Line: Science and the Case for Animals*. Cambridge, Massachusetts: Perseus Books.

————. 2000. *Rattling the Cage: Toward Legal Rights for Animals*. Cambridge, Massachusetts: Perseus Books.

Zurlo, Joanne, Deborah Rudacille, and Alan M. Goldberg. 1994. *Animals and Alternatives in Testing: History, Science, and Ethics*. New York: Mary Ann Liebert.

*Acknowledgments*

KIND, SUPPORTIVE PEO-
ple have always stood behind me as I've researched and written my books, and this one is no different. I would like to thank
just a few of those who helped me:

First, Sally Wofford-Girand, my agent, believed in Bea
right from the start. Then Wendy Hubbert, my editor, contributed her usual, highly astute suggestions and insights. Her
assistant, Ashley Shelby, patiently answered my many questions. And my publisher, Joel Fotinos, has sent Bea's story out
into the world where it can be read, and for that I am extremely
grateful.

So many people graciously allowed me to interview them
or found studies, facts, and figures for me. I could never name

everyone, but I'd like to acknowledge a few of those who gave me their time and energy:

Some are associated with organizations concerned about lab animals: Martin Stevens, Jonathan Balcombe, Andrew Rowan, and Leslie Sinclair at the Humane Society of the United States; Neil Barnard, Jerry Vlasak, Simon Katowitz, and Julie Capon at the Physicians Committee for Responsible Medicine; Elliot Katz, Suzanne Roi, and Patricia Haight at In Defense of Animals; Mary Beth Sweetland and Robin Wesley at People for the Ethical Treatment of Animals; Ray Greek at Americans for Medical Advancement; Pat Davis at the National Anti-Vivisection Society; Ethel Thurston at the American Fund for Alternatives to Animal Research; and Diane Allavato at the Marin Humane Society.

Other people who provided information were beaglers: Mary Powell and Trudi Reveira of Powvera Beagles; Bob Boothe and Janelle Holmes at the National Beagle Club; and Mary Keegan of Beaglers of San Joaquin. Barbara Kolk at the American Kennel Club gave me valuable statistics about dog breeds.

Many of my friends bolstered me as I did my work.

At *Animal People*, Kim Bartlett, publisher, and Merritt Clifton, editor, gave me their usual guidance and advice, as well as some material for this book. Their son, Wolf Clifton, inspired me with his bright, young mind. And Cathy Czapla sent me excellent articles about beagles and lab animals. I owe so much to these kind people.

*Acknowledgments*

Andrea Warren got me started right by pointing out what she said was obvious, but what I had not seen: that Bea and I had much in common. Jeff Masson encouraged me with all his beautiful books about animals. Scotty and Vicki Erwin, who have promised to take care of Phoebe if she's ever orphaned, boosted my spirits, as did Clell Bryant, Stephanie von Hirschberg, and Mike Bogart (as always). Mary Beth Saffo sent me books and articles, and Jeanne Crusemann Daniels provided extremely valuable quotes and comments. My junior high school friends Julie Valentine and Kay Nell Shelton Smith heartened me with their love of animals.

Then there are my Bainbridge friends. My writing colleagues, Natalia Ilyin and Janet Livingstone, provided tea and perspective on Friday afternoons. Meg Hagemann introduced me to Beautiful Joe; and Lin Kamer-Walker helped me walk my dogs while we had splendid conversations about the creative process. Henry Aguilar cheered me with his big heart. And Anton Oblak, my next-door neighbor, waved to me from his kitchen window as I wrote at my desk, and generously fed me soup and pasta.

Three Mill Valley friends, whom I've loved for years, showed me kindness still again. Dick Pervier left an animal poem on my answering machine every Friday to remind me of the wonder of God's creatures. Karol Raymer sent me newspaper clippings, delicious treats, and encouraging e-mail messages. And Martha Hannon, my mentor and one of Bea's greatest fans, was always there, as she has been for decades, to lift me up when my spirits flagged.

Jimmy Wolf, the brother I've adopted, e-mailed me every single day and offered his deep and intelligent insights. And, most important, John Bomben, my husband—who took Bea in begrudgingly but grew to love her as much as I did—was my partner in all things as I wrote this book. My debt to him and my love for him are huge.

Kristin von Kreisler is a well-known animal writer and advocate. Author of *The Compassion of Animals* and *Beauty in the Beasts*, she has been a staff writer for *Reader's Digest* and has written for publications including the *Washington Post*, the *Christian Science Monitor*, *Parade*, *Family Circle*, *Woman's Day*, *Ladies' Home Journal*, and *Glamour*. She has been a commentator on animal issues for numerous television and radio programs, a board member of the international organization In Defense of Animals, and a regular judge for the North Shore Animal League's monthly Lewyt Award for Heroic Animals. She lives in Mill Valley, California, and on Bainbridge Island, Washington. She can

*Kristin and Bea*

be reached at www.kristinvonkreisler.com or at P. O. Box 10472, Bainbridge Island, WA 98110.